Lions of the Lyons

*Colorado Cougars in a Modern
Predator/Prey Drama*

Ramon E. Bisque

Published by West by Southwest, Inc., 912 Twelfth Street, Golden, Colorado 80401.

Printed in the United States of America.

Ordering information available at:

http://www.bisque.com/cougar

Or the above address.

Contact the author by email at: ray@bisque.com

Library of Congress Cataloging-in-Publication Data.

Ramon E. Bisque
[Lions of the Lyons – Colorado Cougars in a Modern Predator/Prey Drama]

Local cougars have conducted an outdoor laboratory course in the Colorado Foothills, attended by the author over the past three decades. Lessons were unscheduled, practical, in some cases subtle, and in others gory. One memorable lesson occurred indoors. The course continues, with emphasis on the predator/prey relationship involving the mule deer and the role of humans.

ISBN: 0-9702513-1-9

November 2004.

Table of Contents

PROLOGUE

The realization came on slowly in the late eighties. Unusual and exciting sightings of mountain lions in our rural residential area were becoming routine. The cats were commonly seen in broad daylight and in unusual places, ignoring structures, vehicles, and people. Sightings of females with young also became common.

The author and his family, who own property and homes in the heart of this activity, began to take note of the phenomena and compare notes with others in the less than one square mile area. Defining the situation highlights a trend recently discussed by others in nearby areas and focuses on an environmental problem that begs attention, if not action.

Damage to date has been limited to the loss of pets and domestic animals, but recent events in other parts of North America indicate that danger to humans, although reasonably remote, is not to be ignored.

The author's experiences and encounters are unique. His limited knowledge of cougars was derived from the cougars that co-inhabit the area in which he lives. His outdoor laboratory course lasted for more than thirty years.

The predator/prey relationship responsible for the cougar's new visibility focuses on the anomalous abundance of mule deer in the area.

CHAPTER ONE

GEOLOGY: THE LYONS FORMATION

Cougars are historically and romantically linked to rock outcroppings. Their agility and stealth allows them to take maximum advantage of rugged terrain. That is indeed a factor in our local environment.

In our area, the Lyons Formation is closely associated with the Fountain Formation (Figure 1). The latter is a unit of sedimentary rock layers that have been lifted and tilted from their original horizontal position during the formation of the Rocky Mountains. In some locales the Lyons rock layers are included as a "member" of the Fountain Formation while in others it is prominent enough to be given "Formation" status. The layered rocks of the Lyons were formed when sand dunes and water-borne sand deposits became buried and cemented. Because the layers vary in texture and direction of flow from place to place, the rocks exhibit what is called "cross bedding." Cross bedding occurs when flowing water or wind changes direction while depositing gravel, sand and silt.

In our area as well as in others, the Lyons Unit is characterized by its structural integrity as compared with the more friable rocks of the Fountain Formation. Outcroppings of the Fountain are rounded while the rocks of the Lyons are angular. Fountain rocks break down and form gravelly soil while the Lyons fractures into angular rock fragments.

Sometimes hidden under core rocks of the Rockies that were thrust over it from the west, and in other locales standing above the landscape as a "hogback former," the Fountain Formation is best known in the Garden of the Gods near Colorado Springs, the Red Rocks amphitheater near Morrison, Colorado, and the Flatirons west of the town of Boulder.

Its outcropping follows a sinuous path from the northern border of Colorado south to an area west of Pueblo, paralleling the Front Range of the Rocky Mountains (Figure 2).

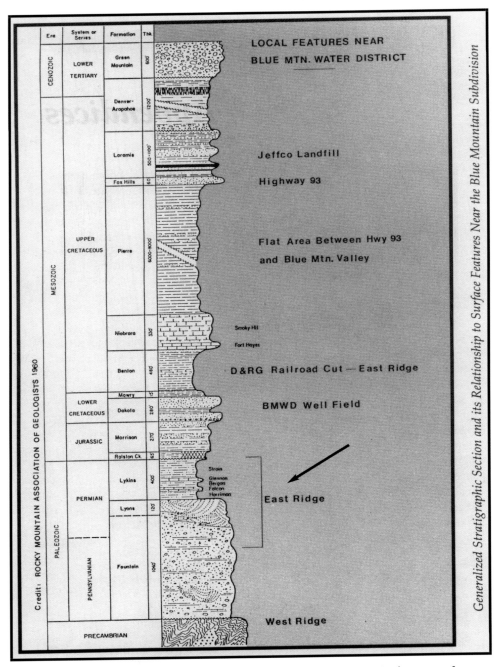

Figure 1: A stratigraphic section showing the relative geologic ages of rocks in the area involved.

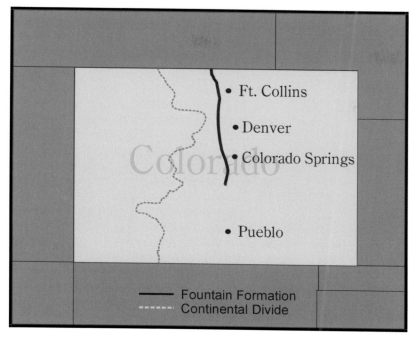

Figure 2: Approximate trend of the outcropping Fountain Formation in Colorado.

Its well-recognized red coloration is due to oxides of iron formed in sediments that were eroded and transported in the geologic past. The texture and cementing of the sands, gravels and clay varies from north to south, resulting in a sedimentary rock that may be friable and easily weathered in some locales and a "monument former" in others.

If one were to start just west of Boulder and walk south along the base of the Flatirons, the rock layers would disappear just south of Boulder and then reappear south of Coal Creek Canyon and Highway 72 at Blue Mountain Valley. Where the red layers reappear south of the Rio Grande railroad they are no longer dipping (slanting downward) to the east as they are at Boulder but are standing almost vertically, actually dipping slightly west. In Blue Mountain Valley you see the underside of the Formation, whereas you walked on the top layers west of Boulder (Figure 3).

This major change was caused by geologic faulting that twisted the rock layers of the formation, breaking and crushing them. That broken zone is where Coal Creek now flows out onto the Plains. The broken and crushed rock has been eroded away, opening a route into Coal Creek Canyon.

Figure 3: Rocks of the Fountain Formation form picturesque outcrops in the valley. The Flatirons in the far background dip (slant) to the east. They dip west in Blue Mountain Valley.

In the upper layers of the Fountain Formation between Golden and Boulder the sandstones are well cemented and resist the forces of nature that work to reduce rocks to gravel and soil. The Lyons Formation is the backbone of the East Ridge at the base of Coal Creek Canyon and supports a habitat that favors the mountain lion. The accounts related in this book took place in the proximity of that habitat, many of them on the rocks of the Lyons Unit itself.

The uniqueness of the rock layers within the Lyons Formation was first recognized by a sawyer, Edward S. Lyon, when he settled in the Foothills in the late eighteen hundreds. Eventually the rocks were used to form patios and walkways throughout Colorado and other states and countries. The familiar "red stone" buildings on the campus of the University of Colorado are from the Lyons Formation. The Lyons rock is typically not as consistent in texture and homogeneity as it is in the area of Lyons, Colorado.

For more details of the locale and environment referred to in this book see APPENDIX A – THE ENVIRONMENT.

CHAPTER TWO

THE SILENT PROFESSOR

Most discussions of the cougar begin by explaining that he has other names. The mountain lion, cougar, panther, painter, puma, and catamount are all the same critter.

The scientific label is *puma concolour* or "puma of one color." In discussing the cougar with foothills residents I was surprised to learn that many were not aware that all of the aforementioned names apply to the same animal. There was also a common misconception of the animal's size. Large males weigh in excess of one hundred and fifty pounds and measure up to eight feet or more from nose to tail. Some confused them with the smaller bobcat and the lynx.

The mystique of the cougar is legendary. Their nocturnal habits, their stealth and their killing ways lend intrigue and mystery to stories. A single sighting can set off a rash of "sightings" and discovery of "evidence" of their presence. They are sometimes "seen" where they don't exist. If you are spooked at dusk or dawn and expect to see a cougar, chances are the first critter you see will look like a cougar.

Old timers hated and feared the cougar. He was killed much as rattlesnakes are killed and referred to as a "vermin." In Colorado, the state paid a bounty for cougars until 1965. In Texas, they are still classified as vermin. On the other hand, the male cougar is the epitome of a loner. His lifestyle prompts many who write about him to anoint him with mystical qualities and place him as an icon of individuality. Naturalist Ernest Seton wrote, "His daily routine is a march of stirring athletic events that not another creature in America at least, can hope to equal."

I never met the cougars that first tutored me. They were always there but until the late eighties I never saw them. I saw their tracks, I found a den and I saw their bloody calling cards on a regular basis. They taught from a distance. There were no lectures, only clues. Knowing that a beast is present and never seeing it is primitive. It is a link to nature.

The instructors were seldom visible but they were always present. Their lessons were subtle but effective. They were infinitely patient as they left clues for me to observe and interpret. With the exception of certain revelations from the books that I will mention, the cougar taught me everything I know about cougars.

My curiosity was piqued when in the late sixties I first came upon a partially eaten mule deer carcass surrounded by loose hair and lightly covered with debris. It was my first encounter with evidence of the cougar and a hint of what was to come.

Back then I was engaged in doing my part in raising a family, working, and traveling. I couldn't spend the time to explore and enjoy our foothills environment to the degree that I wanted but the cougar managed to get my attention. I saw first hand that the cougar hunts alone. I saw "caching" a dozen times before I learned the word. His eating habits were demonstrated via carcasses left on display. With others I watched cougar kittens receiving lessons in dining. I followed the tracks of a mother and kittens in fresh snow and "saw" the kittens cavorting in snowdrifts.

Were it not for my experiences with cougars within a mile of our home, I might well be among those who consider the animal a rare and mythical creature.

***

David Baron, the author of "The Beast in the Garden" (W.W. Norton & Company, Inc. 2001, ISBN 0393058077), discusses recent interfacing of the cougar with civilization west of Denver. Having heard the book was written by a Boulderite, my conditioned response was to assume that it would deal with cougars in the city being tranquilized in trees and carried off to the hills to be released and return again perhaps with a ceremony accompanying each event. The goose-swan-turtle debacle cited later, is an example of the type of activities I had come to relate to Boulder and Boulderites.

My apologies to Baron. I discovered that he is not a full time resident of Boulder. His work is comprehensive and recommended reading for anyone living in an area where the cougar sightings are not rare. I did not read his book until well into this writing and sent Tom Howard of the Colorado Division of Wildlife an early draft for comment. Tom made a succinct recommendation. "I think you should read Baron's book." Baron has done an exhaustive job of documenting local events and interviewing those involved. His "Select Bibliography" section contains some two hundred and fifty sources and "Notes on Sources" is sixteen pages in length. More than a tenth of his pages are dedicated to careful documentation and referral.

His treatment of the Scott Lancaster tragedy near Idaho Springs is moving. I noted that Baron was later quoted in the summer edition of *Boulder* magazine saying that he would no longer hike alone. Awareness of the details of Lancaster's cougar-effected demise would have that effect on a person.

Baron did not mention any personal sightings or encounters with cougars. The discussion herein is largely based on personal experiences and the experiences of neighbors in a one-square-mile area at the base of Coal Creek Canyon, an area referred to in Baron's book.

First Sighting

Marie, my wife, and I did get a glimpse of a cougar in 1956 before we lived in Colorado. I was attending summer field camp as a requirement of studies at Iowa State University. We were living in a tent some one hundred yards downstream from the main facility on the Keaton property in Little Fountain Creek Canyon south of Colorado Springs. A flash flood that sent boulders clumping past our tent prompted us to head for the main camp, an old hotel. A very large cat with a long tail crossed our path and interrupted the beam of our flashlight. We confirmed that there were cougars in the area and thought little more of it. Strangely, the rock formation near the camp, the Fountain Formation, is the same rock formation exposed on our present property.

It would be a quarter of a century before we would see another cougar. We had all but forgotten that incident in Little Fountain Creek Canyon until we began seeing them in our present environment.

While I was otherwise occupied in life's pursuits and Marie was raising our family, the cougars were finding more deer and enjoying our unique setting at the base of Coal Creek Canyon. Over the years there were more calling cards on a regular basis and sightings became more common. I saw my first cougar on the slope above our pasture, less than three hundred yards from our house. It was a magnificent animal that flowed as it walked and leaped effortlessly from rock to rock. I couldn't imagine how people could see a critter and not be certain whether it was a cougar. There is no mistaking that profile and that long tail. As I will relate in the following pages, since 1970 I have seen cougar on no less than twenty occasions, most of them in the nineties. To say that I have seen twenty different cougars would be a different statement. I'm sure that several were second sightings of the same cat. These were not cougars brought to bay by dogs or cougars physically detained in any way, but free roaming, hunting cougars. Some of them were not routine sightings. Read on.

Link To Back Home

I grew up in the Upper Peninsula of Michigan and spent a lot of time "in the woods." Back then we had wolves and stories of cougars. Some of the wolves were brought to town and displayed, never a cougar. I moved from Michigan in 1953 and keep in touch through annual hunting sojourns and the local newspaper. In March of 2001 Mike Zuidema wrote an article for *FUR-FISH-GAME* magazine entitled "Are there Mountain Lions in Michigan."

Although "sightings" are reported regularly, evidence is scanty. Living with the cougar in the Foothills of Colorado, I was frustrated that I had never read an account of anyone in the Upper Peninsula finding a deer carcass with the cougar's calling card. It is as solid as any evidence might be and folks are much more likely to find a cougar-killed deer than a cougar. After reading numerous discussions of possible sightings in the *Iron County Reporter*, I wrote to *FUR-FISH-GAME* to describe the look of a cougar-killed deer. The most salient characteristics are the loose hair surrounding the carcass and the "caching" which involves the cougar pawing grass, conifer needles, twigs, or other debris onto the carcass. Also, the surgical nature of the entry into the vital organs is unmistakable.

Just before this manuscript went to press I visited Iron River Michigan and found color folders published by the Michigan Wildlife Conservancy entitled "Living with Cougars in Michigan". The agency asks residents and visitors to report cougar sightings. I was surprised that criteria for identifying a cougar-killed deer were "teeth marks in the neck" and "caching." There was no mention of the loose hair pulled from the fresh carcass. In all of the cases that I viewed cougar kills, I have never noticed the teeth marks in the neck, nor has anyone I have spoken to. They are not obvious and not something you would usually see without moving the carcass. The brochure does not mention or describe the surgical nature of the entry to the vital organs in a fresh kill and the neatly snipped ribs. Whether this is due to sensitivity and political correctness, or the fact that the writer has never seen a kill, would be interesting to know. In any event, the lack of detail does not serve the purpose of the brochure.

My hope was that information about the loose hair would be meaningful input to the cougar controversy in the area where I grew up. It is obvious and unique.

When you visit the website of the Michigan Wildlife Conservancy, you encounter the following introduction.

> Cougars in Michigan. "We proved they are here. Will you help protect them?"

Those words, "we proved they are here," and the following paragraph caught my interest.

> "Cougars never disappeared from Michigan, but people thought they did. The Michigan Wildlife Conservancy boldly demonstrated, in the face of criticism, that cougars still live and breed in Michigan. With official recognition, cougars can receive the research and attention they need."

This sounded like one side of a controversy. I went to various web sites and discovered that there is indeed a heated controversy about the presence/absence of a breeding population of cougars in Michigan. It has progressed to the point of investigators using DNA analyses of scat collected from various sites. The most recent sighting was discussed in an article by Eric Sharp, a free press outdoors writer in an article dated July 27, 2004. It involved videotape taken in a field in Monroe County, Michigan. The Michigan Wildlife Conservancy sent the tape to a video analysis expert who determined the size of the "large cats" to be consistent with two cougars. A video analysis expert went so far as to estimate the length and weight of the cats. Ray Rustem, who heads the Michigan Department of Natural Resources (DNR) endangered species program, was not convinced, citing other types of cats and technical problems with the video.

My familiarity with the situation in Colorado would prompt me to believe that the controversy will continue for some time.

The mythical nature of the animal is apparent when you analyze the details of sightings. One sighting leads to another. That would be expected if a cougar frequented an area but I believe it is the case even in the absence of the animal. That's a part of the mystique of the cougar. Standing in our pasture in the Foothills of Colorado, a neighbor, another member of our family and I were looking at the steep slope that rises to the east. It was a clear day and the sun was overhead. Cougars were on our minds. A fox appeared and moved laterally across the slope, stopping and starting as he watched us. I pointed and said something like, "Look at that." The fox was a regular visitor and was following a familiar route.

Figure 4: Fleeing animals can be difficult to identify.

"Wow," my neighbor exclaimed, "Look at that. A cougar!" He continued, "Look at that long tail." I knew the gentleman well enough to suggest that he clean his glasses, but he continued to see a "cougar." I suspect that many sightings are of that nature. One of the most classic is well documented by David Baron. It is as follows. A lady near Boulder saw a cougar after she discovered a deer carcass near her home in a subdivision. She complained to authorities and was bothered that the Division of Wildlife didn't do anything about the lion. Michael Sanders, a gentleman who knew something about cougars, visited with the lady and asked questions about her encounter. She had taken pictures. As he left he asked if he could borrow the negatives. The lady had given the photos to a Boulder, Colorado newspaper, the *Daily Camera*. They printed one of them to complement their headline, "Young lion prowls area in Boulder." A legitimate sighting with proof.

Shortly thereafter, a hiker encountered a lion and submitted not a photo but videotapes to Denver's Channel 7. When Michael Sanders saw the broadcast he recognized that the "cougar" was a fox. The News Channel and the local newspaper retracted their stories, but the two events, one genuine and the other a gigantic error, had Boulderites talking about cougars.

I suspect that some of the "sightings" in Michigan's Upper Peninsula may be of the same nature.

If you looked at the photo of the fleeing animal in Figure 4, would you identify it as a cougar? Is it instead a large domestic cat, or a fox? The answer later.

Overhearing a conversation in a restaurant in July of 2004, I checked the morning paper to read the article on cougars the participants referred to. Referring to the town of Fort Collins, the headline read, "Residents worry over 8 cougars in area." The opening sentence stated, "At least eight mountain lions have been spotted in a residential neighborhood on the west edge of town since late May, stirring concerns among neighbors but leaving state wildlife officers with few options."

It is very likely that the eight sightings involved the same cougar, yet the article is written so as to ignore that possibility. It does not mention any multiple sightings. This type of reporting is sloppy, if not irresponsible, yet it is typical.

The plight of "Boulderites" in dealing with cougars, more comprehensively in dealing with nature, is well developed in David Baron's book. It is difficult for some to deal with the truth that we have upset nature's balance and there are consequences. Residents lured "bambi" into their yards and when the cougar appeared they approved of officials sending them on their way with rubber bullets with no thought of where they might go.

The "adventures" of Boulder's "environmentalists" have often been the subject of frivolous discussions. The following excerpt is an over-simplified version of a predicament that was well publicized in Boulder and then commented on in the *MOUNTAIN MESSENGER*.

> ONCE UPON A TIME. Once upon a time some Boulderons became perturbed at the many geese that hung out in their beautiful pond. They imported swans to keep the geese away. The swans luxuriated and procreated. Then an evil turtle ate a baby swan. The Boulderons kidnapped the turtle and his friends and took them away to another land. The Boulderons were scolded by authorities for kidnapping the turtles. The geese are unhappy for being chased away, the swans are unhappy for having been put in peril, the turtles are unhappy for having been moved and the Boulderons are unhappy because they haven't made anyone happy. The end.

It's hard to pass up an opportunity to chide the folks from Planet Boulder. Having originally written the paragraph cited above I have taken the liberty of changing "Boulderites" to "Boulderons."

***

A neighbor, Mark Adams, who spends more time outdoors than I and rides horses while assisting ranchers in the area, has seen cougars on as many occasions if not more. Mark and I have shared information on cougar observations and experiences for more than thirty years. Viewing from their back porch, his family has seen cougar on the slope of the ridge above our pasture on several occasions. I have never seen a cougar while on horseback, while Mark has on one occasion when two cougars crossed Blue Mountain Drive.

The mule deer population in our area fluctuates, but has significantly increased since the seventies. Today, it is not uncommon to drive a mere half-mile in our residential area and see two or three herds of deer averaging ten or more. On an occasion two years ago in October there were three herds, each exceeding twenty in number that hung out on lawns and pastures for weeks.

When I relate my cougar experiences to those not familiar with the Colorado foothills setting in which I live, I can feel and understand the incredulity. Fortunately, I have garnered other observers on numerous occasions and benefited from the availability of friends with cameras. Mark Adams has agreed to let me print his photos and to take some additional photos of sites. Other neighbors who have taken photos or videos in our area have agreed to let me use them and are credited.

Many of the excellent photos of mountain lions have been taken in captivity, or more commonly, after the beast has been treed or cornered by dogs. Beyond that, one investigator used an automated set-up with infrared light and a motion-activated camera to film cougars at their kill during the night. The complex physical set-up was in contrast to the subject matter being photographed and the intrusion seemed unnatural.

None of the photos we are presenting were taken under such conditions. They were all of cougars roaming our area and usually taken by folks who grabbed whatever camera and lens was available.

I am not an expert on the subject of mountain lions but I have never encountered another person, save perhaps Mark, who has seen more cougars on more occasions over a longer period of time. Those experiences span three decades and continue today. Without photographic evidence and other witnesses I would understand why this book would be suspect. I wish that I had kept a journal over the years with locations, dates, and time of day but that is not my nature. On many occasions I cussed myself for not carrying a camera. When I did, I never encountered an opportunity.

I was well into the writing of this book when Mark handed me a copy of Dennis L. Olson's book "Cougars: Solitary Spirits," Northward Press, Minocqua WI, 144 pages.

The book contains great pictures. More than half of the pages are superb color photos, many of them from a film production. Olson includes the research of Gary

Powers and has made a very significant contribution in understanding the cougar but concludes, "We just don't know much about cougars." When he stated that he had seen wild cougars in their natural environment but twice, I was spurred on and went back to organizing my accounts.

Reading Olson's book and the accounts of others convinced me that we in the Blue Mountain residential area are in a very unique situation. None of the sightings or incidents described took place more than two hundred yards from homes. The sheer number of sightings and encounters may be unprecedented. I am certainly not going to add anything significant to the cougar research done to date, but I'm sure that our unique setting at the interface of civilization and the wilderness, and the many opportunities we have to observe their habits, will be of interest to some.

My outdoor, practical course in "cougarology" began sometime in the eighties and continues today.

Some of the discussions might be considered a bit gory. The cougar is a very efficient predator and lives by his hunting prowess. I apologize for the graphic descriptions of killing and the photos included. One cannot ignore such details in discussing the cougar.

Déjà Vu: Another Carnivore

While my lessons were unfolding I was taken back to my boyhood when in 1948, I set out to trap another carnivorous predator, the lowly weasel, recognized in society by the name given its winter coat, ermine. I knew nothing of the small beast except what I had learned from its tracks in the snow while on snowshoeing treks.

I discovered when he was active, where he hid, where he hunted, his victims, and his viciousness. My many trips to "the woods" in pursuit of the weasel brought me closer to nature. When I witnessed the lightning demise of a squirrel after a fresh snow, I was struck by the speed and efficiency of the killer. I intervened and separated him from his bloody prey. When he reappeared and hissed in defiance, I backed off in respect and watched him drag his victim into an opening under a log.

After some success in trapping his kind, I was prompted to put my eleventh grade English Composition lessons to test and submit an article to *FUR-FISH-GAME* magazine and share my adventures. When it was published in 1949, I was on my way to believing I was an author.

I am surprised that other writers have not mentioned this tiny carnivore when writing about the cougar. He hunts alone, is agile and vicious, and will take advantage of domestic animals such as chickens. Other than size, a major difference is that he can be baited with carrion. I used chicken entrails.

The similarities in teaching techniques used by the cougar and the weasel have left me with details of indelible memories and unforgettable lessons. I enrolled with Professor *mustela erminae* when I was seventeen and Professor *puma concolour* in my fifties. Neither of them has ceased his teaching. Three years ago, while four-wheeling on the Flattops in northwestern Colorado, we spotted a chipmunk on the road ahead of us. A flash of brown appeared and opened the throat of the poor creature, ignoring the oncoming vehicle. When we emerged from the truck, the weasel retreated momentarily, and then returned to stand over his prey and challenge us with defiant hissing. Déjà vu.

CHAPTER THREE

EARLY ENCOUNTERS

Our first "encounter" occurred in 1964 when Marie and I were scared half out of our wits by blood-chilling screams in the middle of the night. We had just moved into the area and there were a mere dozen homes in the one square mile. The cries came from the rocky ridge to the east of us, on a property that we would subsequently purchase. I stepped outside not sure what we were hearing. It had sounded like a woman screaming and Marie was heading for the telephone. Standing in the dark, I listened intently and recognized the unmistakable cries of a cat, not unlike an alley cat, but with much more authority. I convinced Marie that it wasn't a human and she joined me to listen. It was the kind of scream that prompted you to stay close to the open door. The cat was probably in the rocks across our pasture, a distance of two hundred yards from our house. Those night sounds, echoing in our silent valley, were hair-raising, if not bone chilling. Years later, I was told that my description of the sounds describe the "caterwauling" of a female cougar in heat. If she was seeking a mate, my bet is he showed up.

I was busy making a living in those years, and hadn't yet purchased the several land parcels that we eventually dedicated in a Conservation Easement. I did, on occasion, encounter a deer carcass, absent the vital organs and most of the choice cuts, and surrounded by loose hair, but at that time didn't make the connection with the cougar. My outdoor laboratory course was about to begin.

I must interject at this point that we have never again heard a cougar scream at night in the four decades following. At the time, there were no homes on the East Ridge. Considering that the cougar has favored this habitat during the past decade after the building of a road and ten homes on the ridge, it surely would have been prime cat country in the sixties.

In the seventies, when residents of Blue Mountain first began to recognize that there were cougars in the area, one of them, Jerry Papke, had had previous encounters with the cougar when he ranched in Montana. Jerry is a not-so-pretty version of the Marlboro Man. With his thrice-broken nose and gangly frame he always looked like he had just lost his horse. His advice was succinct.

"Shoot the sons-of-bitches."

What he had seen and experienced gave him no respect for the cougar. His advice was out of date, the Colorado Division of Wildlife had elevated the cougar from "vermin" status and there was no longer a bounty. Its new classification as a game animal would require a hunter to purchase a license, hunt only during specified seasons, and cease hunting when the quota for the particular Game Management Unit was filled.

Daylight Kill

On the Fourth of July in 1975, we were outdoors painting our deck in the middle of the day when we heard the pitiful cries of a deer being taken down on the slope of the East Ridge facing our home, again not more than two hundred yards away. We could not see the deer or the cougar. I took a break and walked over to investigate; I found the carcass of a doe, breached at the front shoulder. The heart, lungs, and liver were gone and some of the ribs picked clean and trimmed back. Sticks and grass had been scratched up onto the carcass. There was loose hair surrounding the area. Looking back at the house, there was no doubt the cougar could see us from the kill site.

The cougar can kill quickly by biting into the back of the neck to separate vertebrae and paralyze the animal. I did not notice teeth marks on the neck of the kill. One look at the teeth of an adult cougar leaves no doubt of the effectiveness of nature's equipping him to kill deer. The cries we heard no doubt happened in the time between the attack and the biting.

The next morning, the carcass had been dragged off about a hundred yards where it was better hidden. In two days the carcass was picked clean leaving bones, hide and gut. The flesh from the front quarters was eaten last.

It is difficult and of no purpose to place all of my cougar sightings chronologically but in aggregate they are instructive in the unique habits of the cougar. In retrospect, I wish that I had always carried a camera and kept a journal, but with the help of neighbors we can place most of these encounters a fairly chronological sequence.

In those days, we kept a spotting scope mounted on a tripod on the deck to watch a fox family. They had a den under a large flat rock and we were able to see at least a foot or two into the small cave. They would raise five to seven kits each year. The little ones would play and cavort like puppies while a parent would be off hunting. The Adams, neighbors to the south, could see them as well. When one of the grown foxes barked frantically before daylight, our curiosity was aroused. Not far from the den we found a fresh cougar kill. The male fox had attempted to share the cougar's fresh meal and was killed for his effort. There was no evidence of biting or tearing. It appeared that death resulted from a crushing blow. The fox carcass remained there until nature took its course. The cougar showed no interest in eating any part of it.

I am surprised that neighbors' dogs haven't met with the same fate as they often find cougar kills and investigate. Either the cougar exits when they appear or the dogs don't approach a carcass when the cougar is present or the kill is fresh.

Years later, we again found the carcass of a fox near a fresh kill. Again the cougar ate none of the fox flesh. Apparently, it killed to protect its meal. While talking of fox kills, we also witnessed a dramatic event when one of seven fox kits was taken by a Golden eagle. It was still alive as the bird struggled to fly along the ridge. Twice it stopped to rest before heading upslope. The vixen filled the valley with her frantic yelping. In three efforts separated by brief rest periods, the eagle struggled until it reached the highest rocks on the ridge and then glided off to the east with its quarry. The eagle's struggle was too far from the Adams' vantage point to be recorded on video but we will never forget that event. While on the subject of eagles, I once watched a Golden eagle struggling to gain altitude above the East Ridge with a large snake in its talons. The snake was still alive and struggling.

Had we not been monitoring the habits of the fox family we would never have noticed the incident that morning. The kits played and wrestled each morning and evening until they were two or three times larger than when first seen out of the den. Hearing of our ongoing sideshow, a friend gave me one half-dozen goose eggs. At midday I placed them on the slope just below the den. The kits rolled them around unaware of the treat inside or unable to break them. When the vixen broke them open, she gulped down the treat while the little ones watched. In time they all retired to the den where I'm sure they all enjoyed a regurgitated goose-egg feast.

We enjoyed the annual fox family show until they moved south on the slope about three hundred yards, out of our view. Since then they have moved to a more remote den that can't be seen from the valley floor. I came upon it when I observed fox scat bound by the hair of pine squirrels and the feathers of a grouse. That third den area is in a remote part of our Conservation Easement and we hope it will remain a permanent refuge for the fox. Checking scat over the years, I have never found evidence that the fox has been successful in hunting the black Abert's squirrels that live on the ridge.

Fox-watching led to another cougar sighting. Mark Adams swung his scope to check the den and saw a long tail moving back and forth. The cougar was after the young foxes but there wasn't enough headspace. The alert went out and we enjoyed cougar watching for several minutes.

The dens on the slope facing our homes are spaces under huge flat boulders. A close look reveals a young cougar just to the left of the tree on the fence line. Look again. This is not a mature cougar at a cougar den but a kitten investigating a fox den.

Figure 5: Flat slabs of sedimentary rocks form dens. A juvenile cougar sits next to the tree.

***

I would be curious to hear what members of People for the Ethical Treatment of Animals (PETA) might do if they lived in our environment. Trying to legislate and control the behavior of wild animals would at least keep them occupied. They would come to realize that owls eat mice, fox eat squirrels and baby ducks, heron and snakes eat frogs, and cougar eat deer. Then they would have to face the fact that many humans often eat venison. I have a genuine sympathy for folks who have lived their lives in environments that give them an unrealistic view of nature and its ways.

Year after year, we watched mallards hatch and raise ducklings until they were large enough to begin to stray from the family group. The fox systematically decimated them and we never saw an offspring grow to fly away. At one point, I was tempted to interfere by constructing a woven wire fence around the ponds but realized that it would affect the lives of other animals. When thick clumps of cattails developed in several of the ponds, the ducks found haven and we finally saw a new generation fly after more than a decade. The cattails attracted muskrats that thrived for a time and disappeared precipitously. Although I saw no direct evidence, I suspect the cougars found the new delicacy. As a boy in Upper Michigan, we dined on muskrat while on a canoe trip and found it to be delicious in spite of rudimentary preparation.

CHAPTER FOUR

THE MEETING

In the eighties I was constructing a rock cabin on the north end of the same East Ridge. I was in the fourth year of what turned out to be a five-year project. The stone walls were up and the roof was in place. The openings for a door and several windows sat waiting for attention in late spring. In effect, the structure was a giant cave constructed from the rocks of the Lyons Formation that are available at the site. Some display cross bedding, some fossil raindrop depressions, ripple marks, and others smooth slickenslides that formed when rock layers were moved against one another under intense pressure.

Figure 6: Our cabin sits on a ridge formed by the Lyons and Fountain Formations.

After a heavy snowstorm I decided to check on my project. Because of drifts I couldn't drive all the way in so I walked in, enjoying the beauty of the snow-draped rocks and trees with the Boulder Flatirons in the backdrop. The cabin sits in a remote rocky setting at the end of a private road and is surrounded on all sides by steep terrain. I moved slowly down the hill that drops to the cabin site. I saw fresh tracks off to my right running parallel to the path to the cabin. They were headed toward the cabin. As I approached the threshold, there were no tracks on the ground. They ended on the rocks four feet above the entry level and just to my right, five feet from the door opening.

I stepped across the threshold, just as a cougar bolted from the room to my right and exited the window opening directly in front of me. Even though it had to take a sharp right hand turn at full speed, it made no noise. I recall the flash of a long tail. Sheets of plywood blocked the window openings in the room where it had been. Fortunately, the window in the entry room was unblocked, or the cat would have had to exit through the same doorway where I was standing. That could have been interesting. Having an adult cougar bound past you, close enough to touch, is a memorable experience.

The cougar had entered the door opening by leaping from the rocks, a distance of six or eight feet, and left no prints in the snow at ground level adjacent to the threshold.

I hurried back to the pickup and drove down to get the Adams brothers. I wanted someone to see the fresh tracks of the intruder and thought that possibly with three of us we might move down the ridge to the north and get a picture. We followed the tracks for a couple hundred yards or so and gave up. Walking over angular rocks with a blanket of snow over them was no problem for the cat, but it wore us out. It was a perfect situation for breaking a leg. They took photos of tracks in the cabin and exiting the window. The cat had tracked some sawdust into the snow. The distance from the threshold to the doorway between the rooms where the cat passed is six feet. I wonder how many times members of *Homo sapiens* and *puma concolour* have found themselves in such close proximity when neither planned for it.

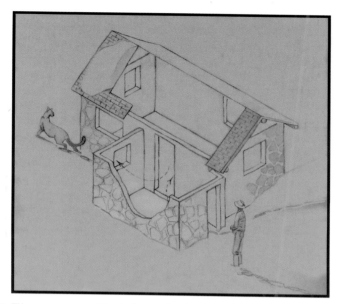

Figure 7: The cougar exited through the north window as I entered the doorway from the south.

What conditions permitted my approach to within feet of the cougar? I was walking very slowly in deep snow and the pregnant cougar may have been snoozing. Perhaps she had just dined and was in the same state as the "Gourmand" described later. Her instincts might have given her a feeling of security in the rock "cave." The cougar is said to be fond of caves and abandoned mine tunnels.

I had chosen the site for the cabin before there was any vehicle access. It was quiet and remote. When the sun warmed the rocks of the Lyons formation and the breezes combed the Ponderosa and Douglas firs there was an aroma that calmed the spirit. Moving over the crown of the ridge one could hear the distant traffic on Highway 72. Moving back to the west a few yards the noise was imperceptible. That is where I would put the cabin. During each visit I would move loose rock to expose the bedrock that would be the foundation of my cabin. The sand grains cemented in the fresh surface of the buried rocks of the Lyons Formation hadn't seen sunlight since conifers were born some 250 million years ago. I left one protrusion of the solid bedrock in place. It extends through the flooring at the north wall of the cabin.

Figure 8: View of the northern end of the East Ridge looking south from the pinnacle. The cabin is visible on the left.

We had rescued the cabin site from a dumb plan of someone in the county government. They had staked a path for a road along the ridge, extending an existing two-lane county road into one of the most spectacular vistas of the area. Bringing that road to county specifications on the steep slope would have decimated a unique area. Some of the large Douglas fir trees on the eastern face of the East Ridge, just below the cabin where the road was destined to go, are in excess of three hundred years old.

Combining resources with neighbors Ann and Peter Luce, we purchased forty acres and petitioned for abandonment of the road. When the petition was granted, I pulled the threatening stakes and began marking a path for a primitive road, avoiding as much disturbance as possible, and ending the threat of any extension to the east side of the ridge. That accomplished, I returned to the cabin site and moved more rocks aside. They would become the walls of a small cabin situated so as not to be seen against the skyline. It was a labor of passion. We moved large rocks with a hand winch and did no blasting. When an area of bedrock was exposed, I shuttled in the first of many bags of mortar and began a five-year project.

The cougar had complemented my choice of the site by her visit. She continued to frequent the area as I pursued my plan. Our encounter in the cabin coincided with the beginning of the influx of cougars in our area. I was to learn later that this decade coincides with the anomalous appearance of cougars in other areas such as British Columbia and California.

Two months after the close encounter and a light snow there were tracks of an adult cougar and two kittens walking the road that I came in on. The adult tracks moved along deliberately while the kittens climbed each drift and rolled down, sometimes in unison. I could visualize the family outing, mom strolling and watching while the kittens' expended energy. I believe that two months earlier I disturbed a lioness that was exploring the "cave" that was to be my cabin. I was surprised to learn that cougars give birth almost any month of the year. I read that this is a result of "induced ovulation," fertility brought on by special conditions.

I have since realized that the encounter in the cabin was a truly unique event and the more I learn about the cougar the more I have grown to appreciate it.

I christened the dead-end ridge road to the cabin "Cougar Lane" and hung a sign near our property line. Within weeks there was a fresh deer kill on the road within thirty yards of the sign.

Figure 9: Marie Bisque prefers an umbrella to make herself "look larger" to deter cougars.

The shake-shingle roof of a small bunkhouse near the cabin can be accessed easily from Cougar Lane. On at least three occasions, cougars have walked to the crest in fresh snow to survey the surroundings. The roof is not a likely place from which to launch an attack. There are two game trails below the structure on the downhill side and the roof is a perfect viewing platform high above the trails. The direction of deer movements would tell the cougar where to go to encounter them. How many times has a cat used this perch when there was no snow to record the event? There are hundreds of perches on the rocks of the East Ridge.

In the seventies I found a cougar den on top of the East Ridge. It was a "cave" under a large flat boulder, four feet wide and six feet deep, tapered to the back. I had never seen cougar scat before and identified it by checking with Danny Harrison, a friend and professional cougar hunter. The den was abandoned when a home was built nearby. I read subsequently that the mother does not use a single den but moves from one to another.

Figure 10: Tracks in fresh snow have revealed that this bunkhouse roof was used as a viewing platform by cougar on at least three occasions.

The large paws of an adult cougar are remarkably effective in deep snow. In firm or crusted snow they keep the cat from sinking very deep and allow it to conserve energy while roaming. I would visualize the cougars as I followed their tracks in fresh snow. With its narrow hooves, a deer in deep snow is definitely very vulnerable. The cougar imprint can be identified by its round shape as compared to a dog print and usually shows no claw marks. The rear edge of the heel pad is tri-lobed. It took me a while to be confident in differentiating the cougar print from large dog tracks, particularly in snow.

The home of Ed and Kathy Moore is on the west slope facing the East Ridge. In 1989 they had a female goat and two kids in their yard. While leaving for an appointment in town, Ed noticed that they had all been killed. When he returned a few hours later at approximately 10 a.m., a cougar was feasting. With a .22 rifle handy, he chose not to go back in the house for a larger caliber rifle and fired six times at the cougar. To his amazement the cougar "jumped backwards" over a fence and walked away. It was found later still alive and dispatched. An autopsy by authorities found the goat remains and included the information that the female had nursed three kittens in the recent past. There was evidence that an automobile had hit it. Not long afterwards their sons spotted a large cougar watching them in the yard and carefully retreated to the house.

Tree Marking

The evidence we have found for cougars included tracks, deer kills, and scat.

Olson and other writers mention tree markings. It's not something that one would notice without looking for them. I will have to be on the lookout. While evaluating a mineral property in southern Venezuela we were in the realm of the jaguar, an animal that holds the same mystique as the cougar. The natives pointed out clear markings on smooth-barked trees that were obviously made with good-sized claws. I thought it curious that the markings were near the ground. They were remarkably similar from tree to tree. The thick, rough bark of the ponderosa and the fir would make it difficult to spot such markings that, I assume, are accompanied by scent. I have never found any tree markings that I could relate to the cougar, nor has anyone I have spoken to.

Camped on the banks of the Pao River, a branch of the Paraqua River in the Orinoco system, seven of us were under the same leaf roof with our hammocks tethered to the same vine-tied framework. I was awakened when my hammock began swinging. Others were awake and talking.

Figure 11: A tree marked by a jaguar near the Brazil border in Venezuela.

A jaguar was walking in a semi-circle around our encampment and sounding off periodically to let us know we were intruding. The sound was not unlike that of the cougar.

CHAPTER FIVE

DINING ETIQUETTE

The Gourmand

Back to cougar events. In broad daylight, sometime in the late eighties, I spotted a large cougar sauntering along the edge of our pasture where the grass yields to brush. It seemed to be oblivious to everything as it moved north for a hundred yards or so and disappeared into a clump of chokecherry brush. I called the Adams brothers and we advanced across the pasture with our eyes fixed on the clump of brush. Mark was carrying a thirty-five millimeter camera and Dave a video camera. The brush was lit by sunlight from behind and the leaves made it impossible to see into it. There was no way the cougar could depart the brush without us seeing it.

We moved closer and closer, becoming increasingly curious. At a distance of fifteen feet or so we were able to make out the form of the big cat lying in the shade. It was looking at us but showed no tendency to bolt. Another neighbor, John Thede, joined us with a camera and we moved still closer. I must mention at this juncture that this event preceded the several disastrous and well-published attacks on humans that occurred some time later. I was not uncomfortable because I could see the cat's face and its prone posture with all four legs to one side. It occurred to us that it might have been sick or wounded. Thede took a close-up photo of the cougar's head. It was the first cougar he had seen.

Then the explanation. The cat had gorged on deer and was literally overflowing at the throat. I would suspect that we were looking at a cougar that had just finished the "first dining" phase of consuming a deer. The heart, lungs, liver and other vital organs along with the flesh consumed to gain access would weigh twenty to thirty pounds and surely glut a one hundred pound cougar. Flies covered the jaws and it snapped at them, annoyed by the pesky cloud. It acted as if intoxicated. I moved in close and shook the brush just as Dave noticed that the battery on his video was dead. Mark was poised and caught the cat mid-leap as it exited to our right. The show wasn't over. It meandered up the slope and settled down behind the trunk of a Ponderosa. Mark adjusted his lens and took another photo. We decided to leave the cat to its digestive process and walked back to the house.

That was the second time I had been within feet of a live wild cougar and my education since then dictates that it will be my last if I have any choice in the matter.

Figure 12: After some prodding, the satiated cougar exited the clump of brush... (Photo: M. Adams)

Figure 13: ...and sauntered upslope to lie behind a Ponderosa. (Photo: M. Adams)

Experts state that the cougar does not chew its food. It pulls off pieces and swallows them whole. After having included the foregoing statement in this manuscript, I watched a PBS special on cougars that clearly showed a cougar chewing. To rationalize the statement with the observation, the "chewing" in the film might better be described as "chomping" or "crushing" and was being performed on a piece of frozen meat.

I can imagine when a hungry cougar gets inside the chest and reaches the heart, lungs and liver it foregoes all table manners and quickly gorges itself, the culmination of patient stalking and a swift athletic maneuver. Judging from what we have seen of a number of fresh kills after the first dining session, those organs are sufficient to satiate an adult and send it off to rest and digest.

Question posed. The fact that the cougar does not chew poses an interesting question. In entering the chest cavity, there are always several ribs "clipped" to facilitate access. There are never pieces of these ribs present indicating that they are ingested. How the cougar can swallow these jagged, broken pieces of rib without chewing them first is interesting. I haven't seen any film of a fresh deer kill being breached. On the one occasion when we watched a dining session (mom with three kittens) the chest cavity had already been opened and the vital organs eaten.

Family Dining

This occurred on the west-facing slope of our pasture near the giant rock outcrop, not far from the fox den described earlier. Someone in our family noticed an adult lion on the slope with a kill. It was a miserable cloudy day with rain changing to snow. As we watched, two kittens came into view. We piled into a vehicle and drove into the pasture where we parked to watch. There were three kittens. The lioness would let one at a time come to the kill and do some tearing. The others kept their distance. If they moved too close it only took a quick feint from mom to send them away. There was no time to waste if the cubs were to make it on their own; there were lessons to be learned. She facilitated the kitten's task by sinking her teeth into the carcass and twisting her head from side to side to partially tear meat and cartilage. When it was another's turn, the exchange was made promptly. The female was a strict disciplinarian. The kittens not engaged in dining lessons cavorted on the slope, sometimes climbing a nearby Ponderosa tree.

Six of us watched with binoculars for at least a half hour until darkness and fog engulfed the stage and the performers became ghosts. Our vehicle was parked in the open pasture no more than one hundred yards from the cougars.

Conditions were dismal for videotaping but the Adams managed some footage in which the cougars can be seen while they move about. The quality did not lend itself to selecting frames for printing. We had seen kittens before but never while engaged in dining lessons. That was a first. Needless to say the entire carcass was picked clean the next morning.

We have never seen kittens smaller than those involved. At birth, they are described as "fist-sized" and they are weaned at two months. The three we were watching were obviously being weaned. There is a significant difference in the amount of meat on a fawn or small doe and an adult. A small doe can be devoured within an hour or two of its demise; a fawn can be easily carried away.

Three days later there was another fresh kill on the ridge not more than two hundred yards from the kill discussed above. There was no snow but tracks of the cubs could be clearly seen in the sandy soil and the carcass displayed evidence of poor table manners.

CHAPTER SIX

READING KILLS

The condition of fresh kills can tell you whether one or more cougars have been involved. The typical one-cougar kill after the first round of dining is shown in Figure 14. Note the area of entry, the missing vital organs, and the clipped ribs. The limbs have not been pulled in different directions as they might be if a second cougar was involved and the hindquarters have not yet been touched. This is indicative of a single cougar in a location where it feels secure, lying down and enjoying its meal. The second dining took the hind quarters and part of the loins. This is a typical "after first dining" carcass. I have seen many that were carbon copies. The big Tom dined again at this site and then dragged what was left to a hidden ledge in the rocks and picked it clean.

Figure 14: A normal dissection performed by a single mature cougar. This carcass had been dragged eighty yards from the kill site.

Figure 15: A sloppy job by juveniles.

Compare the carcasses in Figure 14 and Figure 15. In Figure 15, both the vital organs and the hindquarters have been eaten. It's a sloppy job done by more than one cougar, probably juveniles. The kill was made at night in the front yard of a neighbor not twenty feet from a road and driveway. This photo was taken the next morning. With cars passing during the night they were probably disturbed more than once and gulped their meal. A more experienced mature cougar would have dragged it off to a more "comfortable" area and done a more surgical job.

Many kills in our area have been made in the open away from cover, some of them close to houses. In two instances, Duerksen and Rouse homes, the kills were made within less than fifty feet of residences, one at dawn and the other in broad daylight. A cougar crawling through brown grass is difficult enough to see in daylight and almost invisible at dusk. I have not been able to discern how important the deer's olfactory senses are in avoiding the cougar, but my limited observations would suggest that it is minimal. Deer don't seem to be particularly keen at spotting a motionless cougar, even in the open.

One deer-kill site in a pasture presented a weedy fence line as the only approach route. A twenty-yard sprint took the predator to the prey. Another, in a neighbor's front yard, was twenty yards from a shallow road-ditch that would leave only the top of a crouching cougar's back visible. Since both of these kills were made in the dark, the deer were no doubt surprised by a sprinting cougar launched from close quarters. A distance of about thirty yards seems to be a sure kill range.

George Rouse, a neighbor who lives to the north of our home and nearer the rock outcrops, called to mention the presence of a kill at our common fence. I walked down to see the carcass. It didn't look like a cougar kill. There was no loose hair and the carcass was ripped apart, not dissected. I opined that a cougar was not involved. We didn't have to look far to find bear scat and bear tracks. The question remains whether the bear killed the deer or took it away from a cougar. A bear/cougar tussle would be one of Mother Nature's more classic events.

In March of 2004 our son-in-law Ed Ford and his son heard the unmistakable bleating of a deer being attacked. It was 8:30 p.m. and there was no moon. The kill took place less than one hundred yards from their house. By daylight the carcass was stripped of its flesh and the cougar(s) was/were finished. That "dining" went on during the night in an open pasture and again, must have involved juveniles. The carcass looked like it was torn and mauled. Several cars would have passed on the nearby road. Our three horses were close by, had access to the pasture where the kill was made, and made no audible fuss. I believe a mature cougar would have dragged it into the cover of deep grass a mere fifty yards away. At least one dog track at the site indicates that the condition of the carcass may not have been entirely due to cougars.

On the subject of dogs and cougar-killed deer, our daughter made an interesting observation. During the nineties there were cougar-killed deer in their fenced property on two occasions. Her two Border Collies did not eat from the carcasses. The dogs noted them and walked away. She attributed this behavior to their intelligence, which is understandable with Border Collies. In October 2004, a young doe, obviously a victim of an encounter with a vehicle, managed to jump their fence, or crawl under it through a small hole made by a drainage ditch, before dying. The Collies found this deer and gorged themselves sick. Does this indicate that the cougar leaves a scent that could discourage dogs and other predators?

Yet another kill pattern. In May 2001, Jamie Duerksen was up early to leave for DIA where he would be briefed on the new Boeing 777. Opening the back door, he stepped outdoors and as he turned to close it he looked past the corner of the house to see a cougar straddling what looked like a "big wad of burlap" and was raking dead grass onto it.

Figure 16: Hearing early morning activity in the Duerksen home, the cougar covered its fresh kill with grass.

"His unblinking eyes dialed on me and he didn't even give a hint of leaving because of my presence."

When the lion crouched and hissed at him Jamie realized that it was protecting a fresh kill. He had no intention of leaving home with the lion in the area. He ran downstairs to retrieve a bow and a blunt arrow that he had used to discourage other pests. In his words. "I had to get closer to clear the eave of the house because the lion was on a slope. I did so, making sure that I could get back into the house in case his mood soured. When I drew the arrow back he crouched down over the carcass and flattened himself. This, coupled with the angle of the shot is my excuse for not hitting him squarely. He hissed again. Having just one arrow, I took to throwing rocks and finally got him to move off up the hill. I told Debbie to keep the kids in the house that day and went off to school."

Later he called Mark Adams and Mark called me. Debbie met us in the yard and commented on their visitor. She was completely calm and composed. The cougar had not made itself visible since Jamie left.

Walking up to the kill, I was surprised to see the carcass breached near the back legs. The vital organs were intact. Mark pointed to the explanation. There were two tiny hoofs on the ground; the rest of the unborn fawn was completely devoured including the skull and hide. There was little or no loose hair at the site and an attempt had been made to cover the carcass with grass. The cat shunned protocol and went directly for the womb. The hair at the underside is light-textured and thin. As we dragged the carcass toward the bed of the truck a second fetus slipped out (Figure 17). The cougar preferred the unborn fawns to the vital organs. In a week or two the doe would have probably sacrificed herself to protect the fawns.

Figure 17: The fetus explained the method of breaching.

I got into the cab and began to back up toward a slope where we could slide the deer into the truck bed. Looking through the back window I saw the cougar dart back into thick brush in a draw about eighty yards uphill. It had been watching the procedure. We moved the carcass to a remote location on the East Ridge.

The carcass of this kill had been as thoroughly covered (cached) as any I have seen. The only material readily available was dead grass and it was used effectively. I believe there were two reasons for the caching rather than dragging. The only thick concealment was up a rather steep slope and some eighty yards away. Dragging the carcass downhill would have required passing the house and crossing a road. The closest downhill concealment was at least two hundred yards distant. Hearing activity in the house, the cougar did what was most expedient and covered the prey.

The Duerksen yard was no stranger to cougars. In the 1970's the previous owner of their home, Neil Fox, shot and killed a cougar that had been wounded by a neighbor when it killed his goat. To our knowledge there have been four cougars killed in our one square mile area in the past three decades, three in defense of livestock and one dispatched by authorities after being hit by an automobile.

Months later, as this book was taking shape, I stopped to talk with Jamie about the incident and got the rest of the story. His young son and daughter joined us in the yard. They well remembered the morning when Mark and I hauled off the deer carcass. I had often wondered what that cougar did when we drove off with its meal, containing a rare delicacy. Jamie had the answer. That evening the cougar was still close by, a few yards from where I had seen it disappear into the brush. It caught Jamie's eye as it bounded to a Ponderosa stand to the south and upslope of their house. By the time he retrieved a flashlight and the kids it was full dark. He lit the cougar's eyes with the beam of light and it remained stationary.

Jamie wrote. "The lion had parked himself above the house about seventy yards away at the base of a Ponderosa. His big round eyes reflected the light of the D cell flashlight with amazing intensity. Every ten or fifteen minutes I would go out and shine the light. He never moved or felt threatened. He just waited for me to go to bed so he could continue his search."

The cat was still looking for its lost prey. That conclusion would jibe with the observations of others who have commented on the possessive and aggressive behavior after a kill. Had the cougar stayed in that clump of brush all day long? Would it have been more likely to attack a human after losing its prey? Of all the incidents I will discuss in our area, this one bothers me most. The thought of that cougar sitting there in the dark near a home, waiting to search for its stolen prey is disquieting. It brought back the accounts of the folks who investigated the Scott Lancaster crime scene (Chapter Ten).

When we reviewed the incident, Jamie volunteered to write of another cougar encounter.

"I had driven into Blue Mountain late one night after working the afternoon shift at DIA. It was around midnight and I was listening to a late-night talk show. I crossed the railroad tracks and saw a fox crossing the road. As I approached my driveway I stopped to listen to the radio show. If I had pulled up to the house Debbie would hear the car and then wonder why I didn't come directly into the house. I sat listening with the car idling. In the moonlight I noticed a figure sitting about twenty yards off to the side of my car. I thought it might be a coyote. I grabbed my flashlight, and grinning to myself, thought I'd jump out and scare him good. Guess who got scared? I found myself at short range of a cougar. He went from a sitting position to a lower stance and stared into the beam of the flashlight without blinking. I had one foot in the car and felt that I could get back in quickly if I had to. After a few seconds he bolted across the road. His tail hit the wire fence and he vanished into the tall grass."

These two accounts of Jamie's involved flashlights. It begs the question as to what a cougar can see when looking into a flashlight beam. In the earlier incident behind his home, the cougar had ignored repeated illuminations. In this case, at much closer range, he did not. What is interesting, and disturbing is the fact that the car engine did not spook him in the first place.

When Jamie mentioned that the cat's tail "hit the wire fence" I wondered if it could have been a foot that hit the wire possibly caused by impaired vision due to the exposure to the flashlight beam.

The Duerksens had yet another incident that Jamie believes involved a cougar. Their kitten, an excellent mouser that exhibited an uncanny efficiency that Jamie described.

"She was so methodical in gleaning mice from the tall grass that I thought she must have a vending machine back there somewhere." When the kitty disappeared they found her tail and the Christmas theme collar she wore. The next evening there were cougar tracks in the fresh snow among the vehicles parked near the house.

As I type his story I anticipate that some would conjecture that the small cat might have been a victim of a fox rather than a cougar. This past year our resident fox has had no less than three face-offs with our daughter's house cat. The cat is large and aggressive. Because they involve a domestic cat, a distant relative of the cougar, those face-offs are worth describing. There was no physical encounter, just a lot of serious challenging and threatening. At times the fox would advance while the cat retreated and then the situation reversed.

Information posted by the Colorado Division of Wildlife and other sources state that cougar kittens are taught to hunt rodents after they are weaned, and Olson's book has pictures of a small cat with a mouse. I have never witnessed that activity but there is little reason for questioning published information on mountain lions. They have been common in many states and countries and observed by many people in a variety of environments. Olson and others report that the cougar dines on a variety of small critters including mice, porcupine, ducks, and game birds. Perhaps the fact that we have so many mule deer in our area explains why we have never witnessed, or found evidence, of the killing of these smaller critters.

When seen motionless and lying down, the cougar looks cuddly. Its soft-textured fur and it kitty face would be akin to a teddy bear. When it gets up and moves the image changes. The stealthy stride, long, lean body and keen awareness just don't add up to cuddly.

Following a fresh cougar track after a spring snow I was surprised to see that the cat walked out onto ice, then across several feet of water that was more than a foot deep and continued on. It could have easily jumped the distance. Olson's book reminds me that the cougars in Florida probably spend half of their time in water. In that area the wild boar is a common prey.

Cougars in Florida are a member of a subspecies that is easily recognized by a facial profile that is flatter, and less kitten-like, than the mountain lion I know. Development has concentrated the Florida cats in a limited area and their population is carefully monitored and controlled.

Big Tom

The "notch" between giant rocks of the Fountain Formation is described elsewhere. Our son Stephen was out walking his dog after a snow when he came upon a fresh kill near our gate at the lower end of the passage through the notch. He came to the house to call it to my attention. The tracks of the cat were huge and the doe was good size. The cougar had dragged it upslope for a couple hundred feet and placed it in a depression caused by erosion. The bloodstains on the snow were fresh, the amount of loose hair was minimal and the carcass was breached at the shoulder but almost completely intact. The tracks were as large as any I have seen, measuring at least five inches across. Steve had disturbed a large Tom at the beginning of his meal.

I had often contemplated hunting for a cougar on our land. When they become more brazen I would like to play a role in reminding them that humans can present a danger. I have eleven grandchildren in the area. The Wildlife folks control the cougar population by allowing a limited number of kills in an area. They wisely sell as many permits as folks will buy but then require the hunter to call in the morning of the hunt to see if there are any permits remaining for the area. I called in to find that the area was still open and drove in to purchase a permit. Within an hour of Steve's discovery I was working my way up above the north side of the notch to pick a vantage point from where I could see the kill. Dressed warmly, I hunkered down and waited.

After two hours I headed back to the car and went home for some hot coffee. I lingered and returned to my perch a couple hours later. I settled down again and looked through the scope. The carcass had been moved and more flesh was eaten. I circled around the rock and went to the kill. There were more fresh tracks and it was obvious that the cat had his second helping. I sat at my perch again for a couple hours and gave up for the day. When I returned early in the morning nothing had changed and there was still a good amount of flesh on the carcass. I was surprised that he hadn't returned during the night. This was perfect. The cat would surely be back. After three bone-chilling hours I went home for breakfast and came back within forty-five minutes. The carcass had been dragged up into the trees and then onto a shelf in the rock outcrop where the beast could return unseen along the ridge.

I concluded that I was being watched while I was watching. It gave me that primitive feeling that so many writers describe.

I could find no vantage point any reasonable distance from the new site and I knew that if I moved the carcass my chances would be slim. I decided to wait for another time and another cat. I checked the carcass the next morning and it was picked clean. I have never seen a kill last more than three days before it was left for scavengers.

Danny Harrison, the professional lion hunter mentioned earlier was amused at my one on one attempt to hunt the cougar.

"That Tom is a lot smarter than you are, old man."

While I was occupied with my lion hunt, two neighbors, Ann Luce and Bob Kropfli, reported seeing a very large cougar. It crossed the road in front of Ann while she drove along the East Ridge and appeared just outside the picture window of Bob's new home tucked away in the rocks. Bob measured the distance between front and hind tracks in the snow and reported it was fifty-eight inches. That would exceed what one would expect from the largest cougar but the spacing would depend on what the cougar was doing.

Like the Kropflis, Fred and Clara Tschiffely live in the middle of the East Ridge "cougar freeway." Tucked back in the trees and nestled in the outcropping rocks, they have seen cougars "at least a half dozen times." Fred is the only person I interviewed that actually witnessed a kill. Several deer came charging past him from north of his yard. He walked slowly in that direction and other deer were mulling about. In a flash a cougar was on a large deer and "put it down in nothing flat." Fred watched as it did a quick job of caching and left without breaching the carcass. The carcass was eaten over a period of a few days.

In August of 1999 Diane Kropfli was driving where Blue Mountain Drive intersects the East Ridge Road just south of Tschiffely's and saw four cougars convening on the driveway of a neighbor's yard near the top of East Ridge. She had a camera and managed a picture through the windshield of her vehicle. Viewing this photo with four cougars and the Newman photo with five, both on driveways, a friend wondered if there was something attractive about the warmth of blacktop. I believe that the explanation lies in the fact that these two groups would never have been spotted if they did not happen to be out in the open. You normally won't see a motionless cougar in grass or brush unless you are aware of its presence and looking for it.

Cougars are usually hunted with trained hunting dogs. When a fresh track is found the dogs follow the cat by scent until it climbs a tree or is cornered. Officials that respond to attacks on humans are usually able to find the culprit within a few hours. Other hunters have been successful in attracting cougars by using the sounds of a small animal in distress. The cougar population is carefully monitored and controlled. A successful hunter is required to notify the Wildlife Division of his kill, and bring it to them for inspection and sealing. As mentioned earlier, when the quota for an area has been filled, further hunting is not permitted. Since the cats have no natural enemies to keep their population in check, hunting is essential.

In reading I found that my nemesis, the "Tom Cougar," is a species alone. In his most intimate encounters with the female he gives her but a week or two including meeting, courtship, the honeymoon, and a farewell wave of the tail. He is on his way to protect his territory from any other male that might be seeking status and is willing to kill to remain dominant. The female finds a remote lair in which to give birth, nurses the kittens with supercharged milk for three months, and then teaches them to hunt, all on her own.

On another occasion, in broad daylight in August of 2000, the Rouse family was alerted by a cry from the east side of their home nearest the rock outcrops. Hastening to the end of their deck they watched a cougar drag a doe toward the creek. Twin fawns accompanied the doe. Unusually deep grass provided cover for the cat to stalk his prey within yards of the house. The kill was dragged into thick brush at the base of the outcrops of East Ridge. George has always resisted cutting that great stand of natural grass on his property, but I'm betting that he might change his mind. The fawns separated and one of them crossed the road and in attempting to jump a woven wire fence in my son's yard entangled a leg. Steve ran down with a wire clipper and set it free. George recalls that a cougar killed one of the fawns shortly thereafter.

The kill that took place later in the Rouse's yard demonstrated that the cougar would prefer to take the doe, and let the fawns escape. A much larger dividend for a similar effort. The doe was probably easy prey while focused on her twins.

Within the same week, Chuck Haraway, who lives next door to the Rouses, heard a deer scream and watched a cougar drag it into the same brushy cover along the creek. Chuck and I sat on his deck that afternoon and caught a good look at a cougar as it returned and headed slinked down into the thick brush. Mark joined us with his camera but the cat never came out where we could see it.

The brushy slope on our side of the East Ridge is part of the area in which our horses are fenced. There is never any question when a bear is on the slope, a common occurrence in the fall when the chokecherries are at their ripest stage. The horses stand at attention and focus on the bear like radar units. They are spooked by bear scent and we have to be cautious when riding along the bottom of the drainage in the fall. On the other hand, they don't seem as concerned about the presence of a cougar unless they hear the cries of a deer being taken down.

***

Mark Adams checked with local ranchers and we have found no incidents of horses being killed by cougar in recent years.

One of the photos taken by Mark shows a cougar waiting patiently for deer to graze toward it (Figure 18). It sat patiently and motionless near a rock outcrop, its head barely moving, its ears swiveling. When you looked away and then back it took a moment to focus on the cat again. Mark also took the photo of the fleeing cougar in Figure 4.

Figure 18: The cougar is sitting motionless, waiting for deer to graze closer. (Photo: M. Adams)

In the same locale at another time, I watched a cougar behaving in the same manner. There were a half-dozen does within fifty yards of its position. The does were oblivious to its presence and engaged in grazing. I realized that I was watching a cougar in the process of hunting. In this situation it was a matter of sitting and waiting. The hunter was by no means hidden but was by all means stone still.

While I watched, a pair of mallards swooped in and landed on a small pond not forty feet from the cougar. The cat completely ignored the ducks and they were not aware of its presence. When a doe moved within thirty yards or so the cat slowly crouched down and set its back feet in the manner of a house cat ready to pounce on a toy. The doe moved even closer and I was sure I was going to witness an attack. When the cat sprung into the open, the doe bounded directly away from the line of attack. I was surprised when the hunter stopped after a short advance. Its first and second leaps combined covered at least thirty feet. It gave me the impression that it was playing rather than hunting. With the does spooked, the cat walked uphill and disappeared into the rocks.

Had a second cougar been involved and approached from another angle down the side of the ridge, it would be difficult to imagine that all of the clustered deer would have escaped. The lack of teamwork puzzled me. I later read that cougars, male or female, do not cooperate in any organized fashion while hunting. I find that an interesting trait. The Professor had already demonstrated the lone-hunting trait but I didn't catch on.

If you have ever observed a domestic cat gone feral you have some idea of the habits of a cougar. They move from place to place with an uncanny ability to use every object or shadow that might provide cover. They often stop in places where they can't be seen and survey their surroundings. At times they move in slow motion to remain invisible and at others they move so fast as to appear a blur. Imagine that barn cat that appears from nowhere and flashes past you on its way to safety, being a hundred pounds heavier. When attacking a mouse or bird domestic cats are efficient killers. Increase the size of a feral cat by a factor of ten and the strength by a factor of fifty (a guess) and you have a cougar.

Figure 19: Mark Adams spotted this cougar walking in the open in broad daylight. It remained visible for twenty minutes. (Photo: M. Adams)

The photo taken by Mark with a telephoto lens is of a large cougar that stayed in our view for perhaps twenty minutes or so (Figure 19). The horses grazed below with no apparent concern. Mark later placed an object at the same spot and determined that the cougar was more than eight feet long from nose to tail.

***

At one juncture I began plotting the locations of kills we have found over the years but realized that I was really plotting the areas where I spend the most time. Further, I have seen kills in the open go unnoticed by neighbors for days, so plotting the locations of kills sighted by others is not meaningful data, and I believe they miss most of them. Most busy folks notice them only when they are very close to their homes. In addition, a mature cougar promptly drags the carcass to the nearest concealment.

With all qualifiers considered, the area on the west slope of the East Ridge beneath the large outcropping rocks is a prime "killing field." The cougars conceal themselves in thick brush and attack when deer graze within range.

Llama Over Venison

While checking with neighbors for this writing I called Tom Lavezzi who lives on high ground to the west of the valley. I was aware that he had lost more than one llama to the cougars. The first time, a cougar jumped a six-foot fence at night, killed a young sixty-pound llama, and jumped back over the fence with its victim. He shot the lion from his bedroom window and reported the incident to authorities. He did not have a permit but the shooting was determined to be legal because he was protecting his animals and the bullet did not leave the property. Seeing cougars regularly, he installed motion detectors and lights and kept them at bay for a time.

Eventually he lost a total of seven llamas over a decade and gave up. He reports that not all of the activity was nocturnal and is skeptical of the oft-spoken premise that cougars do not hunt in packs. He and neighbors have seen as many as four together in broad daylight in the vicinity of his home. Was it a pack or a family? Traveling in groups is not the same as hunting in packs. The latter activity involves the cooperation of two or more cats in bringing down prey. While two or three juveniles might gang up on a small animal while learning to hunt, mature cougars hunt alone and are not cooperative.

Targeting the neck in an attack, the cats were "shooting fish in a barrel" when they slaughtered the llamas.

Lavezzi's llama experiences are a parallel to those of a pair of aspiring ranchers who attempted to raise Australian red deer on Magnolia Road northwest of Gross Reservoir. In spite of a cyclone fence topped with three strands of wire "rising to eight feet high" the "Magnolia Lion" succeeded in dining on the expensive imports. A section of the fence "had been deformed, pressed down as if by a heavy object." As I will relate later, that red deer feast ultimately cost the lion its life when it was tracked, treed, and shot near Gross Reservoir.

There has never been a shortage of deer in the area so one could conclude that llama is preferred over venison. That may not be an accurate conclusion because the llamas were contained and may have appeal to an old or weary hunter.

Another neighbor lost a goat to lions, indicating that they are not averse to varying their diet if a gourmet meal is available. In a sense the cougar is "baited" by new delicacies and becomes more of a nuisance than he might otherwise be.

Depending on circumstances, the Division of Wildlife will sometimes compensate a rancher for loss of stock to any predator that can be hunted with a license. The llama doesn't qualify as a stock animal. The Adams brothers lost two steers to a bears in another drainage to the south of us and were compensated. I am not aware of ranchers in the area losing cattle or calves to cougar in recent years.

If a cougar kills an average of one deer a week as is commonly believed, we have evidence at times that at least two are contemporaneously active in our square mile. That doesn't surprise the folks who have seen three, four and five at the same time.

Our area is between seven and eight thousand feet in elevation, transitional between the higher country that has harder winters for longer periods of time and the foothills where winters are comparatively milder. Heavy snow seems to be an ally of the cougar. Mild winter weather favors the deer by making hunting tougher.

Another question that I have not seen addressed. In my encounters, cougars have never used snow to cover a fresh kill. Absent snow, there is always some attempt made to use grass, twigs, brush, pine needles and dirt, to hide the carcass. I would say that it results in camouflaging the carcass more than hiding it by breaking the outline and dulling the reflectivity of the smooth hair. Why is no attempt made to cover a kill with snow? One possible explanation is that the carcass is easier to drag in snow and the cougar moves it to a preferred site rather than attempting to camouflage it. That is consistent with the number of times I have seen a fresh kill moved in snow before the feast begins. The early morning kill in the notch described elsewhere was made in snow and the sizeable doe dragged up a steep slope for eighty yards and placed in a depression for the first-phase dining. Some small amount of hair was pulled at the kill site and more later in the depression. The kill site was much more visible from a broader vista than the chosen dining site.

Had that kill been made in darkness I would guess that the first dining would have been done before the dragging. We have found nighttime kills in wide-open-area pastures and yards, and all of the vital organs and choice cuts were eaten on site.

A daughter, who lives in the valley, has a burro and a huge potbelly pig among other smaller critters. After a fresh snow they found the pig bloodied and evidence that there was a scuffle alongside their barn. A single cougar track came down from the mountain to the west and left along the same route. It was a small cat and apparently became discouraged with the toughness of the two-hundred-pound pig. Those of us who have volunteered to trim the hooves of that pig on two occasions can empathize with the decision of the cougar. If it had attempted to snap the neck of the pig as it would with a deer, it probably discovered that its jaw hinges were challenged. The throat of the short-legged critter is only a few inches from the ground and access would require a unique maneuver. The burro joined the fiasco with frantic braying and attracted attention.

I believe the encounter was with a young inquisitive cougar out on his own and looking for excitement or an easy meal. The tracks, not quite three inches wide, indicated that he walked directly to the area with no stalking or hiding before he dropped from a retaining wall and entered the barnyard for a scuffle.

From my observations and experiences I would categorize three hunters. The first is the adult male veteran who picks a site safe from humans, moves unseen, strikes quickly and efficiently, and drags the kill to a preferred area close by. The second is the female who is raising her family. Her baby-sitting and feeding responsibilities, particularly when two or three cubs are involved, keep her on the go. She is less cautious at times and will kill in less secluded areas if the deer take her there. The third is the brazen young cougar that is curious and still learning. They are not as wary of humans and are learning the hard way. When they become hungry they have less patience.

A fourth category, one that I have never encountered, would be an injured, crippled or very old cougar that can no longer hunt as it might desire. These are the unpredictable killers. Research of others indicates that the loss of essential teeth would cause a mature cougar to take advantage of any opportunity and exercise less caution. Gary Powers tagged a fifteen-year-old cougar that weighed 180 pounds. The cat had recently broken all four canine teeth, essential killing tools. Six months later he tranquilized it again and it weighed 76 pounds. To our awareness neighbors haven't seen examples of physically-impaired cougars with the exception of the female killed by Ed Moore.

Following fresh cougar tracks in the snow is an adventure. They sometimes stroll deliberately and in straight paths. The young cats wander and check everything out. A mature hunting cougar shares it's stalking with you by leaving its trail. When they move among the rock outcrops, the shortened view makes one skittish. Elsewhere I described the trails left by a mom and two or three kittens after a fresh snow.

On Easter Sunday of 2004 with fresh snow on the ground I walked down into the pasture to see if the ponds were collecting water. The snow was firm and dusted with a half inch of powder. A young cougar had wandered up the valley along the streambed, zigzagging and snooping. Greg Pachello, a new neighbor, had asked that I call him when I found a fresh cougar track. I shouted to my son-in-law who was outdoors and asked him to call him. Greg appeared in minutes and we began backtracking the cougar.

"How do you know it's not a large bobcat?" Greg wanted to be assured that he was seeing his first cougar track. No sooner had he posed the question, there in front of us was the telltale imprint of the long tail dragging behind the animal. It had dusted a trench in the surface powder. The tail would touch the snow when the cat climbed from the streambed and up the bank. Greg smiled. He got his answer from the cougar. I smiled. I witnessed someone else who had just learned from the Professor.

***

Lavezzi's accounts caused me to again focus on characteristics of our residential community. Homes are scattered with the average lot size in excess of five acres with brushy drainages and depressions that provide cover. Folks that live in those scattered homes are friendly and neighborly when the occasion dictates, but they keep to themselves otherwise, and stories as unique as those he related don't always get around. After my conversations with him I realized that most neighbors probably were not familiar with my experiences either. I garnered new impetus for my writing and decided to talk to more neighbors.

CHAPTER SEVEN

GROUP PHOTO

Just before sunrise on September 3, 2001, Dennis and Pat Newman, neighbors to the north of us, were preparing to travel on a photo safari to Kenya. Their bags were packed and Dennis had his video camera ready to go. They looked out the window to see five cougars sauntering along their driveway a few yards from a main road. The event rivaled anything they saw on their safari. He managed a full three minutes of taping, with several seconds in which all five were in the same frame. Since the tom never remains with the family, this group of five poses a question. Is it two lionesses with their juvenile offspring or a lioness with four, perhaps two each from separate years? Other neighbors have seen four cats of the same size at the same time. Quadruple births are not unheard of.

The coincidence of the timing, the grouping, the lighting, and the ready access to a video camera resulted in the photos below (Figures 21 and 22). The author is indebted to the Newmans for their use of the video. I'm being redundant, but without ample photographic evidence, many of the stories in this book, including mine, would strain belief. The Newman property is just south of the Duerksen property referred to elsewhere, and on the opposite side of the ridge.

Some light was shed on the nature of this group when I spoke with Ron Bausch about his sighting on that same day. Ron lives next door to the Newmans. Two hours after they videotaped their five visitors, Ron observed four cougars heading east from the same area. He described them as a mother with three juveniles.

They crossed Blue Mountain Drive and the female jumped over a four-foot woven-wire fence into a neighbors yard. The juveniles were not able, or at least not willing, to jump the fence and after poking their noses at it dozens of times they moved to the south where they were able to enter another neighbors property, and headed east, skirting the obstacle. Bausch watched from his vehicle for several minutes and did not see the second adult.

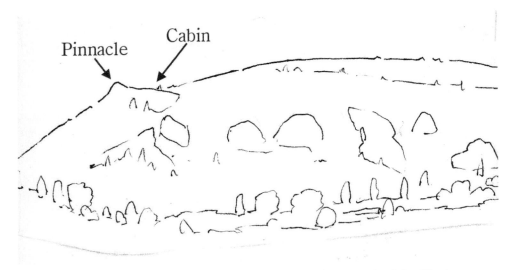

Figure 20: This David Adams sketch (and on facing page) of the East Ridge looking from the west, shows the pinnacle, the cabin, the notch, and the road climbing the ridge on the south end. NOTICE. All land is private property.

Figures 21 and 22: These frames from the Newman video show a group of cougars moving about in full morning light.

It is surprising that none of the juveniles were ready to attempt to jump the four-foot fence. Their size and movements in the Newman video would lead one to expect that it would be no problem. Their nose-poking maneuver might indicate that they were accustomed to going under the wires of a typical ranch fence.

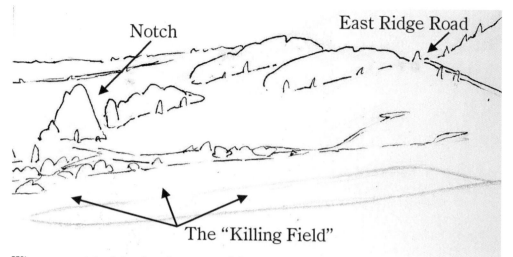

Notch

East Ridge Road

The "Killing Field"

When we watched the female cougar giving her three kittens dining lessons (see "Family Dining" on page 34) one of them displayed great agility in climbing a Ponderosa tree, yet these juveniles did not attempt to jump the four-foot fence.

Where were the cougars between the time that Newman made his video and the time they were seen by Bausch two hours later? There is thick cover within a hundred yards of the two homes that connects with the cover behind the Duerksen home.

Watching the video of that group of five cougars move and interact with one another explained the maze of cougar tracks I had observed on the east slope of East Ridge after a spring snow. There were tracks of different sizes headed in different directions and doubling back over previously made tracks.

While talking with Ron Bausch he reminded me of the young cougar that was struck by a vehicle on the road into the Subdivision in the late nineties. The road crosses the area of the old Boyle Ranch mentioned elsewhere. Ron and others had seen a female and three offspring the day before and again that day. Another neighbor, Joe Tamburini, stopped when he saw others observing the injured cougar and reported the incident from his car phone. Sheriff's deputies dispatched the fatally injured animal and Wildlife officers responded to remove it. The person who hit the young cougar did not report the incident.

Ron and others observed the female several times over the next two days when she stayed in the area searching for the kitten. At times she was seen alone and within two hundred yards of the accident scene. She did not take her loss lightly.

***

Multiple Sightings

Tom Lavezzi and his neighbors watched as many as four cougars on more than one occasion. The Newman sighting of five is described above. Ron Bausch watched four of that same group for several minutes. Diane Kropfli photographed a group of four in a different time frame. The Adams and the Bisques watched a mother and three cubs for more than a half hour. Mark Adams observed two adults crossing the main road in the valley. Observations in our area would suggest that cougar triplets are not uncommon.

Trails

There are definitely established areas used in their sojourns. Mark and I would agree on the location of one north-south route that coincides with the East Ridge and an east-west route across the valley that takes advantage of brush-filled drainages on either side of a ridge that runs down into the valley from the west. The deer kill described on the Duerksen property is adjacent to that ridge.

The fact that they prefer certain types of terrain and cover through which to travel does not offer much in terms of predicting behavior. The intervals between visits to an area, the time of day, and the time of year seem to be random.

Baron cites Don Kattner's effort to determine habitual paths and haunts of a cougar in the Gross Reservoir area. It resulted in a map displaying "Travels of the Coal Creek Canyon/ Magnolia Lion. " The various points used to establish the route all involve the locations of attacks on domestic animals. One might suggest that the map should instead be labeled "Results of live-baiting of a roaming cougar." In fact, six of the locations used to draw the route of the lion are labeled Terrier, Doberman, Labrador, Red Deer, German Shepherd, and Labrador!

To suggest that it is a map of human activity and its effect on cougar habits is certainly not unreasonable. At the time, folks in Coal Creek Canyon referred to a dog on a leash as "A meal on a string" and pets were referred to as hors d'oeuvres.

An "X" on the same map marks the spot where the Magnolia Lion was treed and killed. Moving out in a circle from that "X" there are dead-end roads to the south, the northwest and the northeast of the death tree (page 136 of Baron's book). Otherwise, his "travels" as plotted on the map pretty well follow the density of man's roads. The cougar made a statement in his last hours.

Many moons ago as a young geochemist specializing in analytical chemistry, I learned that the most careful and exhaustive analysis is no better than the sample that was collected. If the sample is not representative of the whole, conclusions based on the analysis are misleading. The sampling of cougar "events" in constructing the travels of the Coal Creek lion are certainly not random nor are they representative of the whole. They are biased by the intervention of *Homo sapiens.*

***

Coyotes frequent our area and I have never seen any evidence of a cougar/coyote encounter nor has any neighbor reported such a meeting. I would guess that the coyote is smart enough to avoid a brawl with a cougar. Coyote experts often refer to them as cowards. I have seen coyotes at cougar kills long after the cougar has taken everything it wanted.

Wild turkeys move about our area but to my knowledge no one has ever found the remains of a kill that might have involved the cougar. Turkey hunters would not be surprised. The keen eyesight and hearing of the wild turkey, along with their organized alert system, would make them a difficult quarry even for the cougar.

Raccoon, bobcat, muskrat, porcupine, and skunk frequent the area but we have never seen any evidence of an encounter with a cougar. Numerous writers state that the cougar is skillful enough to kill and dine on porcupine. Small groups of elk visit our area in the spring and stay around until calving time when they head back into the high country. Newborn calves would be prime cougar prey. The visiting herds stay out in open country where there would be minimum cover for the cougar.

***

Question posed. In our area, crows and magpies quickly find road-killed or hunter-killed deer carcasses. I have seen them arrive at a fresh kill within a half-hour. The same is not true for cougar kills. Fresh cougar kills in the open often lay for days without a crow or magpie showing up. I'm not certain that my experiences make this a valid observation but mention it here to see if others might agree. It may be that cat scent discourages the feathered scavengers but that doesn't seem to hold for the fox. Olson conjectures that the birds are kept away by hiding the carcass. My observations suggest that birds don't visit a cougar kill even in the open until after the second or third dining. This is a very subjective observation but I have seen a difference in the arrival of birds at road kill or a hunter's kill as compared to arrival at a cougar kill.

Since magpies have no sense of smell, their late arrival at a cougar kill might be explained by the fact that the cougar's effort at "caching" may provide enough camouflage to make the carcass difficult to spot. Road-kill or a hunters kill on the other hand are usually quite visible.

CHAPTER EIGHT

LOOKING BACK: COUGAR SIGHTINGS IN OUR AREA PRIOR TO THE EIGHTIES

"One cougar sighting in forty-six years by folks who worked outdoors! That is in sharp contrast to the present situation."

As we look back and recapture events, cougar encounters began to increase dramatically in the late eighties and early nineties. Prior to that time I encountered fresh kills a few times each year, afterwards an average of at least one a month. Other evidence exists. During the seventies, a neighbor, Ann Luce, had a goat that roamed freely at times. We recall rescuing the ungulate from precarious sites on the face of steep outcrops where it stood and exercised its vocal chords. I believe that her pet wouldn't last a week at present. When I reviewed past issues of the *MOUNTAIN MESSENGER*, the January 1990 edition discussed the encounters of the Overmeyers who lived in upper Coal Creek Canyon. Those encounters are discussed in detail in Baron's book. The cover of that issue of the *MESSENGER* indicates that folks were not yet as familiar with the cougar as they would become. It displays a sketch of a lion with stripes!

That time period happened to coincide with my retirement from a Professorship at the Colorado School of Mines and I attributed my increased encounters to the additional time I was able to spend on our property. We had moved into the area in the sixties and our six children roamed and played in the very areas I have been talking about. Our experiences and observations gave us no good reason to fear the cougar. There just weren't that many around. Evidence for their presence steadily increased during the following decades as the deer population increased. Most of the personal experiences I have reported occurred in the eighties and nineties.

My neighbors concur with the timing of the spurt in cougar population in our area. To check on earlier decades before our area was populated, I spoke to Murva Ann Rodgers, daughter of Leavitt and Clara Booth, early settlers. Murva Ann and her brother George grew up in the valley and lived in the exact spot where our present home is located. Murva Ann recalled that there were some sightings in adjacent areas and cougar kills were found on occasion but it was uncommon to see one. She summed it up. "My dad would not have allowed us to roam as we did if he felt there was any danger." Her mother Clara, 95 years young, concurs. Murva Ann and her husband Duane live on high ground to the west of the valley and provided us with photos they took from their hot tub and the photo of a cougar on their deck looking through the screen door (not shown).

Figures 23 and 24: These cougars visited the Rodgers' home on the west ridge in March of 2002, again in daylight.

No one could convince Murva Ann that things haven't changed. She would be the first to tell you that there weren't as many deer in the area prior to the sixties. When we interviewed her father Leavitt several years ago, he related that they often kept a milk cow in the notch where it was easily fenced. I would guess that a cow restrained in that natural corral at present would be in great peril. I have recently found no less than three kills in that "corral."

Her brother George will tell you that rattlesnakes were much more of a concern in the thirties and forties. There were still a significant number around when we arrived in the sixties. The rattlesnake population has declined precipitously. There is no doubt that humans have brought that change about. Few hikers, cowhands or ranchers would allow a "rattler" to live if the opportunity presented itself. The fear of snakes seems unparalleled and they are easily dispatched.

An aerial photo taken in the late thirties reveals a surprising change in the ecology of our area since that time. There were far fewer Ponderosa trees and more open areas. Prompted by that photo, I looked back at our photos of the notch area taken in the sixties. All of the large Ponderosa trees between the rock walls have grown since then. More recent aerial photos show the vegetation trend very clearly. One could logically conclude that the cougar would favor a range with more large trees to climb.

The Boyle family ranched at the base of Coal Creek Canyon for forty-six years, from 1934 until 1980. Johnny Boyle sums it up as follows.

"We knew they were around when they spooked the horses but we didn't see them. We took extra precautions when the mares were foaling. In the seventies I watched a pair come down toward the creek (Coal Creek) from the north off of Red Hill at the base of Coal Creek Peak but other than that we didn't have any encounters."

One cougar sighting in forty-six years made by folks who worked outdoors! That is in sharp contrast to the present situation.

He recalled that Robert Ruff, a builder who constructed several houses in the Blue Mountain area mentioned seeing cougars on several occasions. One of those houses is our present home. When Marie and I were cruising the foothills looking for property in 1964 we met Ruff and visited with him. The subject of cougars did not come up in our conversations but as mentioned earlier, we weren't in the home for more than a year when we heard the screams of a cougar during the night.

There is no doubt that humans are in large measure responsible for the increase in the number of cougars in our area. Firstly, humans concocted the game laws that limit the killing of deer and cougars. That is what they intended to do.

Secondly, humans legislated the laws and the means of establishing protected Open Space areas to protect the natural environment. When they chose to eliminate hunting in those areas, the deer population flourished. When the deer population flourished the cougars moved in. The natural environment was altered.

With thousands of acres of Open Space surrounding our rural residential area we are living in the "happy hunting grounds" of the cougar. We are on a virtual island in a sea of dedicated Open Space in which hunting is prohibited. If the Division of Wildlife continues to be held on the sidelines, that situation will be maintained. I am hoping that the nonhunting aspect of these areas will be revisited. Ideally, naturalists could assume that the danger to humans from cougars in our area is minimized by the over-population of deer. Good theory, but little consolation to parents with youngsters.

Olson refers to M. Hornocker's study on the deer/cougar relationship.

> "...populations of the predator and prey fluctuate together. But the fine point is that the prey population goes up or down first and the predator population follows. When the deer population went up, so did cougar populations. When deer numbers went down, the cougars did too. This has become almost an axiom among biologists who study predator-prey relationships, when a predator has a primary species of prey and is not flexible enough to switch to another species easily, the prey numbers will always dictate the number of predators."

> "So no matter what, "those wolves", "those grizzlies" or "those cougars" are never going to eat all the deer and elk. It won't happen. It can't happen."

> "What does happen is this: Cougars do seem to have a tempering effect on wide fluctuations in the deer population, flattening the peaks and valleys; cougars reduce competition for food among deer by eliminating some of them, therefore improving the condition of those which remain alive."

Hornocker published an article on the cougar in *National Geographic* magazine in November of 1969 entitled "Stalking the Mountain Lion to Save Him." Even with awareness that his study is aimed at saving the cougar, pictures of the beasts with tags around their necks and tattoos in their ears is somehow diminishing.

One of his captions reads,

"…the mountain lion now hangs out in areas where man rarely ventures."

Thirty-five years later, in 2004, he probably would not make that statement. Indeed he might say the opposite.

Baron quotes another writer and cougar expert Edward Abbey, who in 1970 referred to the mountain lion as a creature whose modus operandi, is to observe without being observed. He wrote.

"Only the very lucky ever see this beautiful monster in the wild."

Hornocker's study was made in an Idaho Primitive Area. I would conjecture that the time period of these normal fluctuations would be altered by the impact of human activity such as hunting, ranching and encroachment. Those are factors still being evaluated by ecologists. My experiences with the cougar are part of this new aspect and environment.

The statements quoted above give sad testimony to the changing situation of the cougar. In 2004 the cougars in our area hang out where man lives, works, exercises and raises children. They kill deer within short distances of homes and roam among vehicles.

The elk is a member of the deer family and is a prey of the cougar. Hornocker states that more than half of the elk taken by cougars are calves or very old animals. I have talked with game officers who believe that the toll of newly born calves taken is much higher, but some of that is due to bear. A mature bull elk would surely be a challenge for a lone cougar. When an 800-pound bull elk swings his sharply pointed antlers, they are a lethal weapon. Pick up an elk antler and imagine using it as a weapon if your arm was as powerful as the neck of a bull. Little more need be said.

***

Mark Adams, George Rouse and I have talked of estimating the number of cougar kills we have found over the years. Restricting our counts to the elongate area in the bottom of the valley at the foot of the rock outcrop, we would conservatively say that there are ten kills per year that have been found. If you assume that we have found half of the kills in that small area, which is unrealistically optimistic, that would account for 500 deer since 1980. Even with the consideration of that area being a popular hunting ground, that is a lot of venison.

Looking at it another way that harvest would support ten cougars, assuming they need the nourishment of one deer a week. Because of the wide hunting range of the cougar, this is a flawed statement, but it provides some perspective. A lion tranquilized and tagged in Boulder, Colorado was identified several months later in Manitou Springs, eighty miles south of Boulder.

CHAPTER NINE

POLITICAL CORRECTNESS AND A NEW PROTOCOL

The land that is sketched in Figure 20 includes eight legal, vacant, building sites that we did not wish to develop. Due to increasing land values in 1997 we were faced with paying ever-increasing property taxes. Because our intent was to keep the land undeveloped we looked into the possibility of placing it in a Conservation Easement. We understood that the only right that you forfeit is the right to develop the land in any manner. You can continue to utilize and enjoy it as you did prior to the Easement. In our case that included hiking, hunting, grazing of horses, target shooting and horseback riding, as well as cougar viewing.

When I received the first draft of the paperwork the following paragraph was included under "Prohibited Uses and Practices."

> Hunting. The hunting, possessing, using, discharging or carrying a weapon, trap or net or any means of taking wildlife.

Not only a poorly constructed statement but to us an unacceptable restriction. The young attorney that I spoke to had routinely included the restriction. He didn't have a clue regarding hunting. I stated that we were not interested if this restriction was mandatory. I explained that we had hunted on the land for thirty years, target practiced, and had a weapon in the cabin because of the presence of bear and cougar.

My argument was basically that the Division of Wildlife controls hunting and issues licenses and there was no need for any redundancy by the County. It was obvious that the folks I was talking to knew nothing of hunting and hunting regulations.

After some discussion and several typed versions, the following was included.

> Hunting and Weapons. Hunting, and the discharge or use of any weapon, trap, net or any other means of taking wildlife unless done by the Grantor and the Grantor's guests and invitees pursuant to a valid hunting permit and according to the rules of the Division of Wildlife and any other relevant governing bodies under the laws of the United States and the State of Colorado. Notwithstanding anything to the contrary contained herein, the right of the Grantor reserved in this paragraph is for the Grantor and the Grantor's heirs only, and does not inure to the benefit of the personal representatives, successors, or assigns of the Grantor, unless such personal representatives, successors, or assigns are the Grantor's heirs.

With six children and eleven grandchildren, that clause accomplishes our intent. My point in including this discussion is twofold. Some folks may assume that restrictions regarding hunting in an Easement are essential. Further it is a prime example of the trend to consider hunting as undesirable. Many folks who don't understand anything about wildlife population control and are inclined to be politically correct, perpetuate that trend. Like the folks who regularly feed wild animals, they have the best of intentions.

The first draft of the agreement also included a statement indicating that our Easement would be open to the public. What a way to ruin a prime habitat frequented by a multitude of natural species! We stated that the condition was unacceptable and it was dropped without further discussion.

Another example in our County, brought to my attention by my grandchildren, further illustrates the trend. In a facility that is visited by thousands of students for educational purposes, there are mounted animals displayed. An accompanying citation declares that the animals were there due to road-kill or deaths by natural causes. There is no indication that animals can be taken legally by hunting with a State-issued permit. Again, political correctness taken to the point of promulgating biased information to youngsters.

On one occasion a well-meaning, misinformed neighbor actually wrote to the Colorado Division of Wildlife complaining of our family's hunting habits. He opined that the size of our family and the hunting that we did each year would seriously diminish the deer population. He had no clue about seasons, regulations regarding sex, hunting zones, etc. Another neighbor called the sheriffs office when he heard a shot. A deputy arrived, asked whether we had a license, and much to the chagrin of the misguided and uninformed informant, congratulated us on the "nice buck." His assumption that we were hunting illegally was an insult for which we never received an apology. The deer was taken on our own property.

I offer no apologies to folks who are "disturbed" by the thought of hunting. On the few occasions when I took the time to converse with friends who fall into that category, I found many of them to be completely, and admittedly, unaware of the statutes that control the harvesting of game animals. I have enjoyed hunting and fishing for sixty of my seventy-three years, the last thirty with my sons and most recently with a grandson. I am willing to understand that some have deep-seated emotions about the killing of game animals if they will understand that I have an equally deep-seated passion to be part of nature through exercising my right to hunt and fish.

There are several other hunters in our subdivision who hunt locally. They do it quietly and without fanfare so as not to upset those who oppose the harvesting of game.

Excluding elk, there are more than three million deer taken by hunters each year in the United States. Estimates of the number killed by vehicles, less reliable, would add a minimum of another million. Those "environmentalists" who would ban hunting are simply out of touch with the Nature they profess to protect. Banning hunting would bring on more diseases from crowding and cause the lingering death of millions of deer, not to mention the potential of new strains of disease affecting humans. Good intentions without common sense are simply silly. The revenues collected for hunting permits are used to study and control the populations of deer.

Bear

In 2001, I had the opportunity to witness first hand another example of the runaway consequences of habituated wild animals. It involved the bear rather than the cougar. We were visiting a friend, Pat McGrew, who among other duties, acts as a game control officer for Vermejo Park Ranch in northern New Mexico. The ranch folks do not allow bear hunting on the thousands of acres. With no other enemies to contend with, the bear population flourishes. That particular year a drought had drastically reduced the mast in the area. Bears were hungry and became bold, encroaching on the grounds where guests stayed. Among the facilities was a fish house where hands clean trout for guests. The odor of fresh fish entrails and general curiosity enhanced by hunger brought frequent visiting bears in close proximity to guests.

Pat was responsible for mitigating the problem. His activities during the few days we visited were something to write about. He would use a foot snare with bait buried in a foot-deep hole to catch and hold a bear while it was anesthetized. One day I accompanied him while we "shot" and then loaded three tranquilized bears in the back of a pickup truck. They were treated with great care including putting drops in their eyes and covering them to protect them from the sun. They were then driven to distant areas and released. While we were there, Pat trapped, tranquilized and prepared five bear for transportation. They are driven to points several tens of miles distant. In total that year he moved one hundred and three

bears! They are tagged so as to recognize repeat visitors. A third visit makes a bruin a candidate for euthanization. The following year, with a normal crop of mast, he moved less than a dozen.

While fishing on the ranch, I was reminded of the same boldness and persistence of the cougar when a bear came within forty feet of me while I waded in a lake and ran off with my three trout that I had placed on a forked stick. Entranced by rising trout I failed to look back at my catch until a movement caught my eye. The large brown had the forked stick in his mouth with the trout dangling. He stopped and looked

Figure 25 A habituated bear waits for a tranquilizer dart to take effect before his pickup truck ride to distant hills. It was this bear's third "trip" but he was spared because of his advanced age.

back as if to thank me and strolled off.

He was habituated, I was not. During that same visit I parked my pickup adjacent to a small lake that was designated for fly-fishing only. Sitting on the tailgate, I began to eat my lunch when I noticed several rising trout at the edge of a weed bed. I abandoned my lunch, floated out to the weed bed and was fast to a large rainbow trout with my second cast. I looked back at the pickup to see a large bear sniffing his approach to the truck. A young couple arrived at a clearing nearby and I asked them if they would see if they could rescue my sandwich. It was too late; the bear had already "snarfed" my sandwich and was eating my orange. They took a terrific picture as he sauntered off and later mailed it to me. That was another habituated bear.

The problem in the area was directly related to the ban on bear hunting as well as the drought. The ranch referred to accommodates hundreds of elk hunters each year over several specified hunting seasons. I would guess that when bears begin reducing the elk herds the bear population will have to be reduced. The only way to do that would be with a hunting program.

The area discussed involving bears is the only place I have ever seen a cougar other than in the Colorado Foothills environment. It was spotted by a friend during the elk season as we moved slowly on a logging road in a vehicle.

Hunting Story

I can't mention Pat McGrew without describing our first encounter. In 1998 I signed up for a guided archery hunt for elk in Vermejo Park Ranch. Catering to a bum left shoulder I decided that I had better arrange for the hunt sooner rather than later, the shoulder wouldn't get any stronger with age.

I had no knowledge of Pat prior to the trip. He is one of those characters that anyone would enjoy hunting with. After two days of scouting we decided to try for a large bull that we had seen on the second morning. We positioned ourselves before daylight, I was at the interface of conifers and meadow with hundreds of yards of open meadow sloping gently to the north. Pat was some 100 yards to the south in the timber, using a cow call.

The bull bellowed from a quarter of a mile upslope just as the sun broke the horizon. When I first saw his antlers, lit by the sunlight, he was moving toward us. The antlers would disappear as he traversed shallow depressions and then reappear, each time closer.

He was on a straight path, bellowing and headed for Pat's location. I had time to get set and judge distances. Twenty yards to that clump of brush, thirty to the boulder, and forty to the next clump of brush. If he crossed somewhere in that range I would have an open shot. Finally after thirty years and a dozen such close encounters with big bulls I was perfectly calm. I was talking to myself. "Don't screw up this time. Just put that arrow where it needs to be." Hearing the bull getting more excited, Pat was sounding more and more lovable.

The bull had to dip down into a depression just before he would enter my range. He stopped momentarily before heading down and I felt that he might have sensed danger. The width and symmetry of his antlers gave me no hesitation about shooting. This was a fine bull.

When his head dipped and he began to traverse the depression to my right, I drew my bow. He came up at a slow trot and headed just inside the last clump of brush, approximately thirty-five yards away. I swung with his movement, allowed some lead and released my arrow, aiming just behind the front shoulder. What happened next seemed impossible. With the impact of the arrow, his chin hit the ground and a lunge or two of his huge back legs sent him into cover. I stood there in dead silence and awe, not believing what I had seen. When Pat emerged into an opening where he could see me I said something like "I've got my bull."

Pat flinched and motioned for me to keep quiet. He and I both knew too well that a bull elk can go some distance carrying a fatal arrow. Pat hadn't seen what I saw. As he approached I spoke again. Pat was provoked at my lack of silence but when I described what happened he admitted that he hadn't heard the bull move after I shot. He congratulated me, and ordered me to sit down while he walked back to the truck for a camera.

I disobeyed and when he was out of sight I walked into the timber to find the bull a mere thirty yards from where he met the arrow. I had misjudged and led the bull by two feet more than intended. The arrow entered just in front of the front leg as it was extended back and did immediate lethal damage. The bull scored 320 Pope and Young. My first hunt with Pat McGrew was a memorable one. We did some trout fishing for the next few days and his wife Jackie fried brook trout for Pat's birthday.

CHAPTER TEN

COUGAR ATTACKS ON HUMANS

"To date, no one in our area has ever been threatened by a cougar."

I include this section to add a realistic perspective regarding the potential danger to humans represented by the cougar. Reading these accounts and others has certainly changed my perspective. I will not be as casual about their presence and would be negligent in not including this section. This is by no means an exhaustive summary of cougar attacks.

In 2003 the subject of cougar attacks on humans began appearing in popular magazines. The May issue of *Outside* magazine includes an article by Elwood Reid entitled "Stalker" in which he describes two recent attacks in which the victims were severely injured but escaped alive and recalls a 1994 attack in which a forty-year old endurance runner was attacked and killed by a female lion. Based on documented accounts and his own observations, Reid opines that children are particularly tempting targets.

The accounts of cougar attacks in Orange County California in 2004 are chilling. A male bicyclist was killed and a lady attacked. She was saved by a friend who held onto her legs while the cougar bit down on her head and pulled in a fierce tug-of-war. A group of men joined in and threw fist-sized rocks at the lion. The female friend literally wrestled the lion, kicking its flanks and screaming at it, refusing to let go of her friend. The victim survived.

These accounts bring back the attack on 18-year-old Scott Lancaster near Idaho Springs in 1991. Scott was jogging when the lion attacked him. He was probably killed there on the trail. His body was dragged 200 yards uphill. When it was found three days later, a team of investigators was interrupted by the appearance of the cougar. The animal was killed by a sniper and an autopsy proved it to be the killer. Its return to the site reminds me of the Duerksen encounter in our Subdivision and the bright eyes reflecting the beam of Jamie's flashlight.

Anyone who lives in cougar country and has become blasé about the presence of cougars should read the account of Scott Lancaster's death and the aftermath.

Another jogger, Moses Street was attacked in Rocky Mountain National Park in 1995. The cougar was discouraged when Street yelled and waved his arms. He used a large tree branch to discourage a second and third attack. He climbed a tree and used the branch to keep the cougar at bay while his girlfriend alerted park rangers.

In 1997, Mark Miedema raced ahead of his parents on a trail in Rocky Mountain National Park. When he was out of sight an eighty-eight pound cougar attacked him. Mark tried to fight off his attacker and died from choking on his own vomit. The cougar attempted to drag him away before fleeing. The lion returned while a National Park Service Officer was guarding the boy's body. The animal was killed later by a professional lion tracker and was found to be a female carrying three fetuses. That same year, a four-year-old boy was attacked in Mesa Verde National Park and survived. Again, the lion was found and killed.

In an attack in British Columbia in 1996, a small lion knocked a boy off his horse. His mother came to his aid and was killed. It is surprising that the cougar would ignore the large horse. It may have been habituated to seeing horses.

To date, no one in our area has ever been threatened by a cougar. As mentioned earlier seven llamas and a goat were killed, and a few small dogs and house cats have disappeared over the years. While growing up, our six children commonly hiked and played in the areas discussed. I am sure that the abundance of mule deer has been their protection. The grandchildren have been instructed to "partner up" and never run on the trails. The partnering may not help. In 1998 six-year-old Dante Swallow was attacked in Montana while hiking with three-dozen other campers, and six year old Joey Wing was attacked as he played with five other children. Both children received terrible wounds. A camp counselor pulled Dante away and Joey's mother drove the attacker away.

My intent is not to record cougar attacks but to remind the folks in our area that it can happen. If you know of anyone that needs convincing, refer him or her to these websites.

http://www.topangaoline.co/nature/lionattack.html

or

http://tchester.org/sgm/lists/lion_attacks_nonca.html.

The latest attack reported occurred in Orange County, California on June 28 of 2004. A twenty seven-year-old woman left her hiking companions to return to a vehicle for her sunglasses. While alone she was attacked by a 70-pound lion. Her friends were able to drive the cougar away but not before it did serious damage to her leg and face. Early reports were inaccurate in stating that the victim was with her three hiking companions when attacked. A seemingly innocuous error, it would infer something quite different about the demeanor of the cougar.

Running, jogging and bicycle riding on trails is definitely not a wise thing to do in cougar country unless you remain alert.

My wife carries an umbrella if she feels uneasy on the East Ridge (Figure 9). Popping open an umbrella is something that a cougar probably would not come to investigate. Sans an umbrella the popular recommendation is to hold a jacket or shirt outspread over your head to appear larger. A son-in-law routinely rides a mountain bicycle on trails in the area. After referring to the websites above, I recommended he ride elsewhere or carry a sidearm.

Others would suggest taking along mans best friend. Because of our life style over the past decades we have not kept a dog, but I believe that it would be a good deterrent as long as one would realize that the dog would be put in the front line in any skirmish. The cougar does not like dogs.

After Tom Howard kindly read and commented on an early draft of this book, he wrote on the cover sheet: "Maybe you should be dead by now?" The comment went beyond humor. When I later discovered that Tom had seen young Lancaster's body I read more into it and changed my attitude toward the cougar.

Some Observations and Conclusions

- ✓ Counsel youngsters not to run or ride bicycles on trails in cougar country.
- ✓ Warn folks who are oblivious to the presence of cougars. They may take it lightly but you have done your duty.
- ✓ If you come upon a fresh kill that is partially covered with grass, sticks, pine needles, etc. and breached at the chest, the cougar left by plan and will return.
- ✓ If you come upon a fresh kill that still retains the heart, lungs and liver there is a hungry cougar watching you.
- ✓ If you heard the kill go down or come upon a fresh kill and the carcass hasn't yet been breached you should go elsewhere.

Tom Howard reminded me to include another suggestion. If you come face to face with a cougar, you will probably live through the experience assuming you don't turn and run. It is the unseen attack from behind that should concern you.

Shortly after having decided to include examples of cougar attacks on humans, I read an article by Gary Wockner in the *Denver Post* (April 10, 2004) in which he amused himself by minimizing the danger of cougars to humans. He certainly has the support and substantiation provided by raw statistics. He ridicules what he refers to as mountain lion paranoia and writes about a fictitious event in which a friend presented himself as bait for cougars and attracted none.

In his more serious discussion he mentions that a friend "walked up on a mountain lion eating a deer" and "it didn't even look at my friend thirty feet away." Hardly an observation worth noting. A cougar eating a deer is not even interested in another deer.

Wockner's article made for good Sunday reading and he constructed it so as not to be taken too seriously.

I am a survivor by nature. I anticipate and contemplate danger and do what is reasonable to protect my family and myself. As I ponder the potential threat to my loved ones, especially the grandchildren, I am grateful to see dozens of deer wandering our neighborhood every day. Then I am reminded that the cougar wouldn't be on my land if there were no deer.

Discussing cougar attacks could lead one to the subject of potential legal exposure in real estate sales. Is the remote possibility of a cougar attack on humans and the more likely possibility of loss of pets or domesticated animals something that should be revealed in a real estate transaction? There are lawsuits based on expanding soils and flood damage, will there be suits based on damage done by cougars? Would mental anguish suffice?

Other Observations in Our Area

Our limited observations in a small area over the years would support five generalizations that are probably obvious by now.

- ✓ Since the eighties, there are commonly sightings in broad daylight.
- ✓ Deer kills are usually made after dusk, at night or in early morning. We have seen two exceptions.
- ✓ Once they are agile, the female often exposes the offspring to civilization.
- ✓ Kills are commonly made in wide-open areas with little or no cover.
- ✓ Human-built structures are no deterrent to the cougars' movements.

***

In the last decade, the average annual cougar harvest in the state of Colorado was 350. In the preceding decade, 157, and in the decade preceding that, the first decade of cougar hunting, 66. This does not necessarily translate to a greater population of cougars since the number of hunters has increased steadily over the three decades. The cougar harvest statistics are not broken down into game-management units.

In 2003, hunters in the game management unit in which we live (unit 38) harvested a total of 439 deer. That unit, directly west of Denver, includes portions of Gilpin, Boulder, Clear Creek, and Jefferson counties and is bounded on the north by the Rollins Pass road (U.S. Forest Service Road 149), Colorado Highways 119, 72, 93, and 128, on the east by I-25, on the south by U.S. 40, and on the west by the Continental Divide, a total of approximately 500 square miles. Assuming that some deer-kills are not reported, the annual harvest is close to one deer per square mile.

CHAPTER ELEVEN

HABITUATION

I was not prone to use the verb "habituation" in this discussion, rather I would have used "accustomed " or "acclimated," but recent usage indicates that the word is "habituated." The first two definitions in my computer dictionary refer to "habituation" as related to drug use, that is, "tolerance to a drug resulting from repeated use." As used herein it refers to changes in habits in response to changes in the environmental factors.

As is obvious in my ramblings, you can't write about the cougar without discussing its prey. In some locales it is the whitetail, in others it is the elk or the mule deer. Our area has exclusively mule deer with the annual brief spring visit of the elk. You couldn't write about grizzlies without dealing with salmon, or the beaver without mentioning aspen but the predator/prey relationship between the cougar and the deer is unique in North America. The deer is also the most often chosen prey of the big-game hunter in the United States. There are seasons to accommodate both rifle hunters and archers. In our state the pursuit of deer and elk results in an infusion of a billion and a half dollars into the economy each year. Each fall we join the cougar in pursuit of a common prey. We use rifles and bows, while the cougar relies on teeth.

We have had unusual opportunities to observe mule deer does with newborn fawns. I include here my article from the *MOUNTAIN MESSENGER* of August 1996.

MAMMA MULEY MATERNITY MANNERS

Four years ago on Father's Day a doe that had been hanging around our yard and using our deck as a sun umbrella, moved into a clump of tall grass and delivered twins. We were able to view the birthing from a window directly above the site. She and the twins stayed in the yard for four or five days before they headed for the hills. This year on Father's

Day another doe delivered twins about the same time of day not more than fifty feet from the site mentioned above. These two births gave us a good purview of muley maternity manners.

Shortly after the first nursing session, she moves away and the fawns sleep. She may be as far as sixty or seventy yards away and seems oblivious to her offspring. Hours later she returns for another nursing session and leaves to browse again. At this stage she eats voraciously, gorging on almost every type of vegetation available including young aspen leaves and Marie's planted flowers. When she lies in hiding to ruminate, she may not be in position to see the location of the fawns, sometimes lying on the opposite side of the house. When the time comes for another rendezvous she walks slowly and alertly with her eyes scanning the yard. Within minutes she finds the fawns and another nursing session begins. The fawns usually begin to stir about the time she begins to look for them. If there is any audible communication involved, these old ears didn't detect it. This year she kept them in the yard for more than a week, ignoring vehicles and noisy grandkids.

During the first days the fawns avoid detection by curling up and remaining absolutely motionless, so motionless they appear to be dead. If they do spook and run they don't have a clue as to the location of mom but she detects the action and steps out to make herself visible. Mom hangs around while the fawns frolic but separates herself when they nap. This year they left the yard after nine days. Now they are back on the ridge where the cougars have a regular harvest. I saw them on the Fourth of July. The family was still intact and the fawns were surprisingly agile on the rocky slopes.

When you analyze this behavior from the perspective of a hunting cougar, it makes sense. The cougar is most likely to spot the mother first and reveal himself in pursuit of her. The fawns are at a distance and wouldn't be aware of an encounter unless, of course, the cougar was successful and she never returned. While she is away they are lying motionless and wouldn't be detected. They are most vulnerable when they are cavorting, even though the mother is usually present. When a cougar devours a small fawn, little remains as evidence, making a count of fawn kill impossible. It is probably quite high. I would guess that if one fawn is taken by a cougar hunting alone, the other escapes with the doe. The frequency of twins in the species might well be an evolved survival mechanism.

Does continue to use our yard as a maternity ward. While editing this section in July of 2004 there are two sets of spotted fawns and a pair of young deer from last year "hanging out" in the yard.

Habituation of the Prey: Examples of Deer Acclimation

Marie has a difficult time growing any flowers that deer enjoy eating. When she moved them onto the deck I had to hang a gate to keep them from coming to the flowers. None of those flowers were available in the wild. I was amazed to see them walk on the redwood deck. When they want shade they lie under the deck on the cool gravel and often don't exit when we sit on the deck. When Marie attempted to shoo them away from rosebushes they all but ignored her and never moved more than a few yards away. We do not have a dog in our yard.

From a distance of twenty feet, I watched one evening as my three horses waited politely while a half dozen mule deer drank from the stock tank. They drank one by one, took a few steps and leaped over the fence. One of them detoured to take a few licks from a salt block before departing.

One lazy sunny morning in May I took a cup of coffee out to the deck and prepared to settle down with the newspaper. As I held the paper and cup in one hand and prepared to move a heavy wooden chair with the other, I spilled half of my coffee. A buck mule deer, with small mounds of velvet, rattled the loose gravel as he headed for the lawn. The spaces between the deck boards had allowed some of the coffee to spill on his ears. He shook off the coffee and grazed along the fence before returning to the shade under the other end of the deck.

When I start up the tractor in the yard, I sometimes drive within twenty feet of deer that don't bother to get up. They often snooze just outside our solarium window and watch motion inside without getting up. Fertilized grass seems to be preferred greenery. The leaves of aspen, cottonwood and other deciduous trees planted near homes provide other variety. Elsewhere I mentioned the fawns that are born in our yard each year, usually close to Father's Day.

Figure 26: Our inner yard, surrounded by a six-foot board fence, has been a maternity area for mule deer. This fawn is one of twins born thirty feet from our house. Does have given birth in the exact same location on at least six occasions. (Photo: M. Adams)

Mule deer seem to be able to eat most any type of vegetation. A neighbor will tell you that they are fond of rose buds just before blooming. In desperation, gardeners have used soap, mothballs, garlic, various stinky concoctions, and other chemicals to discourage hungry does from decimating their plants. My wife will tell you that they "hate" zinnias, shallots and garlic. That is not to say they won't uproot them while investigating. Folks in Boulder have used lion scat acquired from a zoo. I watched a doe dine on a fat cactus and carefully avoid the spines. I was surprised to see them eat fungi but read that it is common. Mule deer regularly browse on the severed branches of mature Ponderosa trees when we thin or prune them. Give that a taste test!

Discouraging deer from browsing in yards has become a popular topic in the foothills. Most folks are not thinking in terms of reducing the prevalence of live cougar bait. They are interested in maintaining the attractiveness of their environment. Frequent articles in the garden section of newspapers and magazines deal with the problem. The mere fact that lawns are irrigated and may include delicious nonnative grasses such as Kentucky bluegrass is a factor.

Trees that are indigenous and easy to grow such as aspen, and Rocky Mountain juniper, are attractive forage. Deer stand on their hind legs and stretch their necks to enjoy these staples. Pruning to a height of six feet helps. We've had little luck with lights and motion detectors or electric fences. Quite by chance, we discovered that they are not fond of Mountain harebell, a long lasting flower that is easy to grow. The attractive Oregon grape and kinnickinnick that grace the East Ridge are not to their liking.

In terms of discouraging the cougar, I doubt that even a concerted effort by all residents in a foothills area would be sufficient to keep deer away. There are always fringe areas of grass that benefit from irrigation, and expanses of pasture areas and lawns where grass is encouraged to grow and deer to graze.

Antler Protection

For at least six months of each year, the male deer is a less attractive prey than the female because of his antlers.

It would be interesting to know how much of a deterrent a set of antlers are to the cougar. With the exception of one buck with small antlers in velvet, we have never found a cougar kill with antlers. The fact that the deer carry antlers for only a part of the year is a factor, but any hunter who has been jabbed by an antler while moving or lifting a buck will understand why the cougar would prefer to attack an antlerless animal. A good-sized rack of antlers flung by the strong neck muscles of a buck would inflict a painful jab. The cougars target, the neck vertebrae just behind the antlers, are well protected. That prompts me to stray for a word or two.

During a fall deer-hunting season when I had drawn a permit for a four-day hunt in November, I killed a 4x4 mule deer. I realize that in the year 2004 I should more properly say that "I harvested" or "I collected" the deer but the fact is that when I harvested or collected the animal I killed it. The buck had an injured leg and the end of its tail was severed, something I had never seen before. Skinning the animal, we found claw rakings on both sides of the hindquarters. We hadn't noticed the marks in the thick hair on the exterior of the hide. The spacing of the claw marks indicated a good-sized cougar. The marks did not extend to the flesh beneath the hide.

I surmise that the backside attack was prompted by the presence of the sizeable set of antlers. An attack on such a big buck also suggests that the leg injury probably occurred before the attack and caused the buck to be singled out. That hypothesis is, however, weakened by the fact that the leg injury was not caused by a hunter's bullet and it is difficult to imagine how a mature buck would break a leg. In any case, the buck managed to escape the attack. If he had not been "harvested" he probably would have had to endure other attacks.

Olson's book indicates that the buck may have been a victim of testosterone overload, which makes sense. I have watched bucks during the peak of the mating season and observed them to be quite careless about their concealment. They don't have an entourage of does to warn them of danger and their minds are on other matters.

Prior to mating season, during the regular designated hunting seasons, the bucks seem to vaporize.

I kept the hide and took it in to Jonas Brothers to be sent for tanning. I was disappointed to discover that the tanning process obliterated the claw marks. Years later one of our burros appeared at the barn with similar claw marks in the same location. Millie, one of our two burros, often ventured upslope into the rocks and presented a unique opportunity. I would guess that an overly-ambitious cougar received a good kick in the groin and decided to go back to deer. In areas of the Southwest, cougars commonly kill burros. I would be surprised if the burros are killed by the technique of biting to separate vertebrae. A burro has a very strong neck several times the girth of a mule deer and a thick padding of flesh. It would seem that they would have to go underneath and attack the esophagus or the jugular.

As mentioned, I have seen but one other antlered deer killed by a cougar. The carcass of a small buck with seven-inch, velvet-covered spikes was being picked clean by crows near Highway 72 in July of 2004. The kill was several days old but the unmistakable pattern of clipped ribs near the front shoulder suggested the puma.

The different shapes of mule deer antlers are certainly a factor in sparring and protection. My sons and I identify antler shapes with a simple ratio. We measure the width at its widest point and divide by the height from the skull at mid antler.

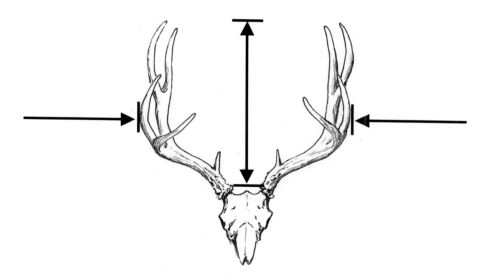

Figure 27: The ratio of the antler width to height varies considerably for mule deer bucks. (Sketch by D. Adams.)

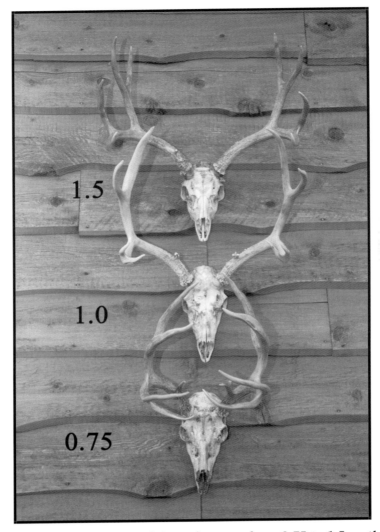

Figure 28: The width to height ratios vary from 0.75 to 1.5 on these racks. (Photo S. Bisque)

A "square" rack, where width and height are equal is a 1.0. It's a quick way to describe shape. In the photo of antlers, the tall rack has a ratio of 0.75 while the wider is 1.5. Ignoring the relative size of the antlers in the photo, there is no doubt as to which type of antler is the better weapon. The tall "closed" rack would be easier to avoid and to grasp. I have bet that these are the racks that most commonly become "locked" in sparring, causing the demise of two male animals. We took two racks similar to the rack with the 0.75 ratio in the photo and "sparred" with them. We were not able to bring about a situation in which the antlers were "locked" to any degree.

Figure 29: Regardless of shape or relative size, we found it impossible to actually lock antlers unless torque was applied and maintained. If both "combatants" relax, the antlers separate. Evan and Daniel Ford demonstrate.

They remain "locked" only when one of the sets of antlers is torqued. Although indicative of shape, that ratio of course says nothing of the overall size of the antlers. I have typical four by four mule deer racks that vary in size from a raw (Boone and Crockett) score of 50 to 200. Both the largest set of antlers and the smallest are "four by fours."

Figure 30: The wide rack of this mule deer (antler ratio of 1.6, 206 B&C) would discourage most predators. Taxidermy by Jonas of Broomfield, Colorado.

We see many young male deer sporting modest racks intermingled with the herds of does and fawns, but the mature males with larger antlers typically remain out of sight. There is a period of a few weeks that corresponds with the early hunting seasons in which large males seem to disappear. They become less cautious in November when the mating season begins.

There are volumes written about mule deer. I am focusing on the "muley" as I know him in the same environment where I met the cougar. They spend time at higher elevations in the summer and move to lower elevations in the winter. In our area, larger bucks sometimes appear or disappear overnight. Since we are at the transition zone from winter to summer habitat as well as the interface of two ecologies, Plains and Mountains, we can expect the unexpected.

Having grown up in the Upper Peninsula of Michigan, I became familiar with the white tail deer. We hunted in fairly thick hardwoods and cedar low lands on typically flat or gently rolling terrain. Hunting the mule deer in the foothills is quite different. The terrain is steep and rocky and cover varies from Ponderosa and Douglas fir stands to open areas of brush and grass. Before cool weather sets in, the bucks will find a comfortable bed in the shade and remain motionless for hours. Their dull coloration blends in well and they are difficult to spot if they don't move. When standing motionless early in the morning or at dusk they seem to disappear. Even in sunlight with a sizeable headdress they are very difficult to spot in thick brush. The mature bucks commonly feed at night.

In our area of the Foothills there appears to be a gene that affects the characteristics of mule deer antlers. They are very wide, "typical" or balanced in symmetry, and have a characteristic small spike or two on one antler. Mark and David Adams pasture steers in a drainage a few miles south of ours and have had the opportunity to compare antlers over the years. They do not see antlers as described above. They are typically narrower and higher. The latter shapes do occasionally appear in our area. They have width/height ratios less than one. I don't know how this observation jibes with studies of the mule deer's range, but it has held for years.

Habituation of the Hunter

"The cougar has become habituated to preying on habituated deer. We must now habituate ourselves to the habituated cougar."

Figure 31: Habituated mule deer in our yard. (Photo D. Ford)

Figure 32: Sunday morning relaxation. (Photo D. Ford)

The cougar can observe these "domesticated" deer from a distance. They are in the open, almost always grouped, and commonly distracted. Distracted in the sense that they become oblivious to motion of all kinds. If a cougar is crafty enough to ignore noise and enter that altered environment he can easily get within striking distance of a comfortable mule deer.

We have altered the habits of the prey and made it easier for the predator.

While on the subject of our inner yard, there has never been a deer killed by cougar on those two enclosed acres in spite of the fact that it harbors deer in numbers that are anomalous even in our area. While I have found cougar tracks on the road adjacent to the yard and there have been deer kills close by, I have never found a cougar track or a kill in the yard. A six-foot fence constructed of redwood boards surrounds the yard (Figure 29 and Figure 31). It apparently gives the mule deer a feeling of comfort but is shunned by the cougar. Having watched cougars move about, I believe I know why. Unlike a wire fence, it limits his visual surveillance and distorts sounds. He would find easy pickings, and there is ample cover for stalking, but the fence barrier impairs his vital senses.

While this manuscript was in its late stages, I looked out and saw a herd of twenty deer across the pasture below the notch. They were in a prime kill area, grazing and browsing from a stand of brush below the notch. Thinking that it would make a fine photo for this dissertation, I called my son-in-law and grandson and we sauntered down toward them. As we approached they decided they wanted no part of picture taking, moved away, from below the notch and headed west. When we got back to the yard some five minutes later, the same group was posed on our lawn, most of them already lying down.

There are areas on the periphery of our residential area where the cougar can find almost complete seclusion in rugged terrain. Rating seclusion on a scale of one to ten, those areas would be at least a nine. The hunting, on the other hand, would be rated a two or three. When the cougar moves closer to our homes, the hunting becomes a ten and the seclusion a zero.

Many folks don't want to disturb the deer or allow human hunters in the area. They are in truth inviting the cougar.

Biologists will tell us that either the cougar will thrive as the deer population is diminished or the deer population will thrive as cougars are diminished. I truly doubt that this law of nature applies in present day Blue Mountain. We are protecting the cougar in vast areas surrounding us and providing more and more deer for their upkeep. At present, with the artificial balance at hand, both species will thrive until some other factor such as disease or new laws intervene. My conclusion is based on what I have learned from the deer and the cougar.

The control and monitoring of deer populations, which are in most part done through hunting regulations are essential to maintaining healthy herds. Since 1981, Chronic Wasting Disease (CWD) has been identified in herds in at least twelve states. Most cases occur in adult animals and are almost always fatal. To date there is no evidence of its spreading to domestic ruminants such as cattle, sheep and goats and no evidence of its having affected humans. As this manuscript is taking shape, CWD is moving south along the Front Range having reached Colorado Springs in May of 2004.

Examples of Cougar Habituation in Our Area

- ✓ Cougars have become comfortable walking among automobiles and being in proximity to them, even when the engines are running.
- ✓ In many remote locales the cougar regularly sees joggers, hikers, and cyclists at close range.
- ✓ They have become accustomed to barking dogs held in restraint.
- ✓ They find delicacies such as cats, goats, llamas, and other domesticated animals.
- ✓ As discussed in this book, they find their favorite prey in abundance in association with buildings and fences.
- ✓ The cougar may spend hours at a time within earshot of human noise including voices and children playing.

    ✓   At night, roads and trails provide easy strolling and a good view.
    ✓   Bright lights that turn their eyes into eerie reflectors don't seem to perturb the cougar.

Habituated by these and numerous other factors, the cougar is not the same as he once was. He has changed in response to his basic characteristics interacting within a new environment.

The cougar has become habituated to preying on habituated deer. We must now habituate ourselves to the habituated cougar.

His habituation is not confined to interaction with the civilized environment. In Yellowstone Park where he is now challenged to live with the newly introduced wolf, the cougar must adapt. He is not alone at the top of the food chain. He must satisfy his carnivorous appetite with a competitor present. Watching a film made in Yellowstone Park I was struck with the effort spent in caching compared to what I have seen. The carcasses are not just camouflaged with a light application of litter, but also actually buried in a heap of debris. I would judge this to be due to two factors, the presence of the scavenging wolf and the fact that much of the prey, such as elk. is large and the supply can last for several days if not found by the wolf.

The Yellowstone monitoring indicates that wolves have killed a half-dozen cougars.

The humans in our residential area are in the early stages of their habituation. In maintaining pets and domesticated animals, they have to consider the presence of the cougar or suffer the consequences. Some, albeit few, are recognizing the presence of the mule deer is the key to the presence of the cougar.

***

Some suggest that dogs are an effective deterrent to cougar comfort. There are many dogs in our area and at times a lot of barking goes on, but I can't say that it has discouraged the wandering cougar from his investigating. The number of dogs that have been killed by cougars runs counter to the idea that they have an inherent fear of canines.

Canines certainly hate cougars. Baron notes an incident in Glacier National Park in 1990 where a pack of eight wolves killed an adult female cougar, tore at the body of the victim, but did not eat it. One wolf was observed urinating on the cougar's head.

On many occasions my activities on the north end of the East Ridge on a calm day will set off a chain of barking in the valley below. I am always surprised at the minimal noise that will trigger the din. The cougar doesn't make noise unless a victim broadcasts its last cries. Dogs that are outdoors respond. Dogs kept indoors among house noises may not hear yard intruders or distant disturbances.

***

Habituated Turkeys

In the last decade wild turkeys have become increasingly common in our area. They can often be heard gobbling from the ridges. The Merriam, or western turkey, is a large and beautiful bird, a treat to see in the wild. In October of 2004 our son Steve crept through the brush to take a picture of a flock of turkeys with his new digital camera. To his amazement, they spotted him, ran toward him, and posed for great pictures.

Figure 33: A habituated Merriam turkey poses for a photo. (Photo: S. Bisque)

The turkey is considered a prime game bird in some thirty states and hunting them is a great American tradition. Stories of their wariness and uncanny elusiveness abound in hunting magazines. Steve had encountered habituated turkeys that are fed regularly by residents of our area. They have been transformed to gobbling pets looking for a handout.

There are those who see this as a desirable condition, bringing nature and man together. In truth, it is a sad situation, altering the basic habits of one of nature's finest wild birds for the enjoyment of observers.

CHAPTER TWELVE

THE TOP OF THE FOOD CHAIN

The cougar has his venison fresh and raw. I prefer mine in chili or as rare steaks taken from the choice cuts. We process our animals and follow extreme care in preparing the meat for the freezer. There is not a trace of any tallow or gristle remaining on the pieces that we grind or package for steaks. At least two thirds of it are "ground" with a rotating dish cutter and frozen in one or two pound packages. Ground mule deer venison is very absorbent and will soak up a lot of liquid during cooking. To make hamburgers or chili we mix it with ground beef. I never "brown" the ground meat when making chili, but simmer it with tomato sauce and beer, allowing spices to be absorbed into the meat. After that we add the tomatoes, beans, green peppers, etc. To our taste, steaks are best cooked rare and enhanced with a balsamic reduction, mint sauce or other flavorings.

We usually have one meal of fresh liver cooked with onions. Mule deer liver is "stronger" than elk liver that is considered a delicacy by many liver fanciers. The first successful hunter at our elk camp is a hero and his prowess is celebrated with a meal of thick liver slices fried with onions.

Our extended family has spent many man weeks hunting elk at high elevations for four decades. In addition, we owned and operated a remote resort on the border of the Flattops Wilderness Area for five years. We have never seen a cougar, much less evidence of a cougar kill, in that remote area.

Most hunters have never had the opportunity, or perhaps the desire, to cook and eat the flesh of a carnivore. I have eaten bear meat on two occasions separated by more than fifty years, and once had the opportunity to taste cougar meat prepared by smoking. The bear meat was delicious. The thought of eating cat somehow kept me from rendering an objective opinion on the taste of cougar. All I could think of was our kitty eating a mouse.

***

In an otherwise over-civilized world, the cougar continues to remind me that there is another world out there. A world where beauty is real, survival an individual matter, and death by killing, routine. I would prefer to have known him in a more natural environment.

Hunting deer and elk with a bow has given me some appreciation for the cougar's skills and takes me away from the complex society that I am a part of. I fear the cougar, but if he leaves I will miss the reality and quality that fear adds to my being.

CHAPTER THIRTEEN

HUMAN COUGARS

In 1976 Lloyd L. Morain, a self-appointed philosopher wrote a book entitled "The Human Cougar" published by Prometheus Books, 923 Kensington Avenue, Buffalo New York 14215. ISBN 0-87975-062-6. Morain says nothing of the source of his familiarity with the cougar but his characterization of humans who have cougar traits reveals that he knew considerable about the critter.

His Preface states that the Human Cougar is an endangered species.

> "Roaming about, free from regimentation, overlooked by bureaucracies, and largely outside of social welfare-systems, he often escapes notice. Yet this outsider is very much a part of American life, and the West as we know it was largely created by this brand of working drifter."

From his acknowledgments.

> "To the hundreds of Human Cougars who have shared highlights of their hard and lusty lives with me I offer warm, grateful thanks. In chance meetings on waterfronts and highways, in rail yards, hobo jungles, orchards, cattle ranches, mines, logging camps, bars, and coffee shops, Cougars have given me insights into ways of life I could never fully experience."

He interviewed several men who were typical cougars and summarized unique characteristics of their lives. One of his paragraphs that deals with the aging Human Cougar is poignant.

> "That is when the dream begins to take shape. Usually it concerns an acre or plot on the edge of a town, somewhere in

the foothills of the Sierra Nevada, in the great central valleys of California, in the backlands of Colorado, Montana, Oregon, Idaho or Utah. You picture yourself retaining your freedom, raising most of the food you need and storing it for winter, working part-time on ranches, and doing a little gold prospecting. You figure out how you could heat a small mobile trailer with a wood-burner and how you can fish in some nearby stream or lake. You have this dream of settling down for once, though basically remaining independent. Sometimes it does happen, but more often than not, the dream is cut short by the onslaught of ill health, the coughing of blood, rapid physical deterioration caused by old injuries, years of overexposure, excessive smoking and undisciplined eating and drinking."

I met Morain shortly after he wrote the book. He gave me a copy because we had a common acquaintance who would qualify as a Human Cougar. I took the book from the shelf and perused it again before finishing this book a quarter of a century later. I have known several of these men in my lifetime and their faces flashed before me as I read Morain's sad analogy. The book meant less to me before knowing the cougar.

EPILOGUE – THE MEETING IN THE CABIN

That was a pivotal meeting in the cabin on that snowy morning in the late eighties. She arrived first, I arrived shortly thereafter.

I represented all of the things that her predecessors had never known; fences, concrete, and blacktop; noise, smells and odors. I represented silvery projectiles that drew lines in the sky from horizon to horizon and cloth wings that floated humans over her hunting ground in the Foothills; buildings with windows that reflected the sun during the day and lit the trees with their light by night. I represented clusters of lights that sit on the slopes and strings of lights that moved along strips that incise the mountains. I represented "ground thunder" that broke rock and made dust as valleys were prepared for permanent flooding. I was the kind who put collars on her cousins and followed them to those special private lairs using telemetry and aircraft.

As she had for centuries, she represented solitude, independence and nature itself. She is primitive. She must kill or starve. Her kind kills and eats "bambi." Her presence is a constant reminder of the realities inherent in the food chain and the ways of nature.

The meeting was brief. There were no minutes to approve, no resolutions to vote on, no coffee breaks, no formal adjournment. Just a brief meeting and she left. She headed north through the fresh snow across pristine rocks to find a place to give birth. I hurried home to describe the encounter.

Her attitude and hasty departure spoke for her kind. My reaction was scripted by our sacred and primitive relationship. Had there been time, I would have been a poor spokesman for my people.

There will be many more meetings on the subject matter. They will be held at universities, in hotels, in the offices of lawmakers and in the courts for decades to come. None will be as brief, concise and effective as that meeting in my cabin. None will involve a cougar. I owe her this book and wish her well.

APPENDIX A – THE ENVIRONMENT

The unique geological and geomorphologic setting in which the events and encounters took place is an integral part of our story.

1. The area in which we live is unique in topography and is contiguous with some very rugged Foothills terrain to the south. Much of the surrounding area is protected Open Space. To the west the terrain begins its climb to the Continental Divide.

2. The property which we own in that area has been a hobby of mine since the nineteen seventies and I have spent a lot of time walking over it and working on it. We recently placed some forty acres of it in a Conservation Easement with Jefferson County. It includes a strip of wetland supported by an intermittent drainage. Small ponds offer water to deer when other sources are dry. The type of cover that exists when grass and other vegetation is leafed out is ideal for concealment.

3. The residences in our area are scattered and provide dozens of excellent vantage points for viewing terrain that cougars inhabit and hunt. Our home faces the East Ridge. Between lays a grassy meadow and a wetland strip that supports brush and sedges providing good cover during the summer and fall.

4. The mule deer habitat is enriched by the fact that we are at the interface of the Plains and the Foothills, and the thousands of acres of Open Space surrounding our one-square-mile residential area is restricted to hunting. Mule deer proliferate. This factor is discussed in detail.

5. The flora varies from that associated with ponds, to meadows and slopes, and includes sparsely vegetated rock outcrops similar to those overlooking Boulder, Colorado. An indication of the variability of habitats is found in the ecology. Referring to a report written by Michael Figgs, an ecologist who was engaged by Jefferson County to perform an inventory when we placed a portion of our land in a Conservation Easement.

"There are five species of trees, twenty-three species of shrubs, seventy-three species of forbs, twenty-five species of grasses, eight species of sedges and rushes and two species of ferns within a quarter of a square mile."

Figgs observed this to be highly unusual. After reading the information in his professional inventory, I found a more technical reason to appreciate our land.

***

In addition to the environmental changes that accompanied the building of roads and homes in our area there have been several others.

In 1976, we filed for rights to impound water in a series of small ponds along the intermittent drainage that parallels the East Ridge. The existence of the resultant wetland zone over the past eighteen years has encouraged the upstream migration of willows and the establishment of cattails. Turtles, muskrats and ducks joined the fauna and zillions of frogs attracted the Great Heron. Deer enjoyed the convenience of the watering holes and the cougar enjoyed the presence of the deer.

In that same decade a major infestation of pine beetles decimated stands of majestic Ponderosa. Volunteers worked for months felling hundreds of trees, sectioning the logs and branches, stacking them, treating the stacks with chemicals and covering them with plastic. In addition many Ponderosa were weakened by heavy growth of mistletoe to the point where they had to be removed. The resultant change in the density of the canopy increased the amount and type of forage for grazing by deer.

In August of 2002 a wildfire ignited by a passing train burned 90 acres of grass and brush on the east face of East Ridge and torched a few dozen large Ponderosa trees. The recovering vegetation is attractive to deer.

A predator that has not changed its habits over the years and makes its presence known on a regular basis is the great horned owl that feeds on mice and voles. It sits on the East Ridge and sends its call out across the valley. Regurgitated pellets of bones and hair mark their favorite roosts. It is amazing how the low monotone hoot carries and can be heard through the walls of a house.

Locations

"Foothills" refers to the ridges and slopes that are at the interface between the High Plains and the Rocky Mountains. In the specific area being discussed the rock outcrops are similar to those seen at popular sites such as the Flatirons west of Boulder, the Red Rocks amphitheatre south of Golden, and the Garden of the Gods near Colorado Springs.

The physical relationship of the rock formations that are the foundation of the East Ridge are shown in the "stratigraphic column" (Figure 1) prepared by geologists to depict the physical relationship of sedimentary rock layers in an area, youngest (top) to oldest (bottom). The relative thickness of rock units are not consistent from locale to locale and depend on the environment when they were first formed.

Blue Mountain Valley

The "valley" referred to lies just west of the first Foothill ridge at the base of Coal Creek Canyon. There are some ninety homes in the one-square-mile area that encompasses the valley. The terrain to the west of the valley rises toward the Rocky Mountains proper.

East Ridge

This rocky ridge runs north–south and separates the valley from the plains. The north end of this ridge is steep and remote. It is characterized by a tall rock pinnacle surrounded by angular boulders that have broken off over the centuries geologists refer to this as "mass wasting." There are openings and pathways through and beneath these boulders where a cougar could den out of sight and have multiple entries and exits. It is extremely difficult to traverse and has no paths leading to it. Our cabin is two hundred yards to the south of the pinnacle at the end of Cougar Lane.

Figure 34: Photo looking south near the notch. Note the more rounded rocks that result from weathering of the Fountain formation as compared to the "blocky" rocks of the Lyons in Figure 6 and Figure 8.

The author's property extends from the central bottom of the valley and includes the north portion of the East Ridge.

The Notch

The notch is an east-west passage eroded through the tall outcrop on the East Ridge. The "walls" of the notch rise two hundred feet above the creek bed and are very steep. This type of erosion is typical of the Fountain Formation. It relates to the original character of the rock. In some places it is well cemented and resists erosion and in others is quite friable. The sculpting of the Formation in forming the Garden of the Gods is a prime example of erosional forces working on a rock unit of variable composition and physical integrity.

Figure 35: This passage, cut through the rock of the Fountain Formation, was used as a corral for cows in the nineteen thirties.

West Ridge

There is not actually a ridge to the west of the valley, but the name of the road that climbs the mountain on the west side of Blue Mountain Valley and the area is commonly referred to as West Ridge. It reaches the first high ground west of the Foothills. In years past, a stagecoach trail wound its way up from the valley and west to Blackhawk, Colorado.

Blue Mountain

The topographic structure, Blue Mountain, elevation 9,322 feet, is actually two miles west and outside of the area being discussed.

APPENDIX B – MISCELLANEOUS EVENTS

❖ Sometime in the late eighties or early nineties, our daughter Camille was on the east slope near the giant rock outcrop to the east of the notch collecting Ponderosa pine cones. She "felt funny" and looked upslope to see a cougar looking at her. The animal was lying down and "licking its chops." Not having been instructed in cougar encounter protocol she left the slope in haste, turning her back on the lion. I believe the cat was in the process of dining and ignored her. I was out of town and no one checked for a deer carcass.

❖ On a warm spring morning when the ridge was bathed in those subtle combined smells of conifers and warm rocks, I was moving slowly along the road to the cabin removing rocks that had rolled from the uphill side of the road cut, a weekly task in the spring. I suddenly had that "feeling" and looked up to see a cougar just below the skyline and fifty or sixty yards away. From the cat's perspective, it heard an occasional click or thump of rocks and probably came to investigate. My legs would have been below its line of sight due to the road bank and my torso was moving along in an up and down motion. The position of the sun made it difficult to see details of the cougar but it looked as if it had stopped mid-stride and stayed motionless while it peered at the creature below. I stepped up onto the uphill slope and the cat disappeared. At the time I considered that event casually and had no discomfort or concern whatsoever. My ignorance of cougar habits at the time fostered a cavalier response to its presence. That attitude has since left me.

Had that been a hungry, mature cougar and I had not looked up to see it, the encounter might have been more interesting. I was moving and was vulnerable in my position on the road and below the grade of the slope. I continued my task with an occasional uphill glance and ended up at the cabin

❖ Walking his Golden Retriever on the East Ridge our son Steve was behind the dog as they climbed through the notch. When he caught up the dog was at the base of a Ponderosa, looking up and barking. As he approached, a cougar leaped from the tree and headed off with the dog in pursuit. Veteran cougar hunters suggest that Steve's approach at the right moment might well have saved the dog from harm if the cougar had any previous experience with dogs.

❖ Hearing my cougar stories, Dr. Patrick McCarthy, a colleague in Golden, packed his children in his car and headed for our area. They drove to the top of west ridge and onto a dead-end road. A mature cougar obliged them and appeared and crossed the road.

Patrick exited the car and looked down the steep slope to see the lion looking up at him from twenty feet away. They would probably have to make that trip a million times to make another such sighting.

❖ From the *Denver Post* October 5, 2004. Kate Wellington of Evergreen, Colorado met with a cougar on two consecutive mornings. While on a morning hike she encountered a cougar in the "blond autumn grass of a ravine. She was within eight feet of it before she saw it. She and a neighbor drove it off. On her walk the next day, the cougar was back perched in the middle of the trail. Wellington had a walking stick and struck the cougar when it "prowled within three feet of her." Neighbor's dogs joined in to chase the cougar away. I include this account from outside our area because it emphasizes an observation made earlier. The cougar is very difficult to see in autumn grass. I believe that Ms. Wellington was fortunate that neighbors and dogs were near. The title of the article was "Cougars under siege from growth." Again the predator was lured by a habituated deer.

❖ Late entry. At a picnic organized for residents of our community in September of 2004, a proud new landowner talked of building their home and described her small pet dogs to one of our family members. When told of the cougars in the area she was surprised and noted that she would provide protective accommodations for her pets. The land they purchased in on East Ridge Road and a few hundred yards from most of the activity described in this book.

❖ Bruce Allison, a close friend, hunts mule deer in an adjacent drainage during the archery season. He attempted to cover his scent by applying elk scent left over from the previous years hunt. He was hunting on private property adjacent to an Open Space area near Golden. Moving slowly along a ridge, he paused when he had "that feeling." Someone or something was following him. He turned his head slowly to meet the stare of a trailing cougar that was no doubt curious about the elk scent. The cat sulked off, disappointed in what it had discovered.

❖ Just before delivering this manuscript in October 2004, Greg Pachello and I walked the "killing field" from north to south looking for cougar-killed deer. We were aware of one that was killed out in the open just east of our residence. Within a half-hour, we found two additional carcasses, approximately one week old. I am quite sure that there will be new "lessons" to write about just as soon as I send this book in for printing.

***

My apologies to cougar experts for any inferences or conclusions that are incorrect. I could have conducted much more research of the literature, but preferred to have this book reflect the first-hand lessons that I received from the cougar.

Additional events will be reported at www.bisque.com/cougar

ACKNOWLEDGMENTS

My thanks to all of the friends and neighbors mentioned and especially to David and Mark Adams for their assistance.

Tom Howard, Colorado Division of Wildlife, for his many useful comments and encouragement after reading an early draft.

Don Ciochetto, owner of the *Sportshop* in Iron River, Michigan, who called my attention to the brochure published by the Michigan Wildlife Conservancy.

To Dan Bisque, for his work in formatting and preparing this manuscript for the printer.

To Eldred Erickson, a high school classmate, Iron River High School, 1949, for his detailed editing.

To neighbors who read and commented on early versions: Mark Adams, George Rouse, Phyllis Thomas, Greg Pachello.

To Mark Adams, Ed Ford and Steve Bisque, for photos taken.

To all of the cougars I have met, especially the female who inspected our cabin.

To Marie, for all of her persistence, patience and understanding.

Note to Residents of Blue Mountain Estates

It would be great if residents of Blue Mountain Estates would jot down the date and location of sightings, deer kills, loss of livestock or pets, etc., for future reference. For exchange of information and ideas please contact the author at 912 Twelfth Street, Golden, Colorado 80401 or by email at ray@bisque.com.

THE AUTHOR

Figure 36: In this photograph taken by Mark Adams in 1988, just after "the meeting," (see page 23) author Ray Bisque stands at the north end of the East Ridge. Coal Creek Peak is in the background to the north.

A scientist by trade, the author has hunted and fished since he was a boy in Michigan's Upper Peninsula. His first publication was an article in *FUR-FISH-GAME* magazine, submitted in 1949 when he was eighteen years old. That same year he achieved the status of Distinguished Rifleman in the Junior Division of The National Rifle Association.

After attending St. Norbert College in Wisconsin and graduate school at Iowa State University where he met and married Marie Livingston Young, they moved to Golden, Colorado where he taught at the Colorado School of Mines. The author's conversion to a "westerner" was immediate and permanent.

Introduction to the mule deer and the elk opened new hunting vistas. Archery elk hunting became a passion pursued for four decades and fly-fishing in mountain streams, a relaxing pursuit.

In the professional arena he is Chairman of the Board of ADA-ES a firm specializing in retrofitting coal-fired power plants to reduce pollution, is Professor Emeritus at Colorado School of Mines, a Fellow of the American Association for the Advancement of Science and a Certified Professional Geological Scientist. The Bisques have six children and eleven grandchildren. A hunting landmark was reached in 2003 when a thirteen-year-old grandson, Danny Ford, bagged his first elk.

In 1991, Dr. Bisque was selected to receive the Native Son Award in Iron County, Michigan.

In 2000, he published *IRON* an historical novel based on court documents, relating dramatic events in the life of his great grandparents after their arrival in Iron River, Michigan in 1883. http://www.bisque.com/iron.

His unique familiarity with the cougar came about fortuitously as a result of the geographic and geologic area the family chose for residence and continues today.

INDEX